Family Visiting in Out-of-Home Care: A Guide to Practice

Peg McCartt Hess
Kathleen Ohman Proch

Child Welfare League of America
Washington, DC

CHILD WELFARE LEAGUE OF AMERICA, INC.,
440 First Street, NW, Suite 310, Washington, DC 20001-2085

Current Printing (last digit)
10 9 8 7 6 5 4 3 2 1

Cover design by Anita Crouch
Text design by Eve Malakoff-Klein

PRINTED IN THE UNITED STATES OF AMERICA

ISBN # 0-87868-344-5

Contents

Introduction

You have been assigned a case involving two children placed this week because they were abused by their parents. If the children are comfortable enough to ask, their first question of you is likely to be, "When can we see our parents?" This is just one of many questions concerning visiting that you will have to answer in this and in every case with children in placement. How often will visits be scheduled? How long will they be? Where will they be held? Will they be supervised? How will the visiting plan change over time? The list of questions is long, and each decision is difficult, requiring careful assessment of risk to children and of parents' abilities to care for their children.

A Guide to Practice will help you answer these questions as you develop and carry out visiting plans. Visits are the heart of permanency planning. Although published research supports the importance of visiting, few resources have been available to assist those who develop and implement visiting plans with this complicated work. *A Guide to Practice* is intended to help those directly involved with children and families develop visiting plans that facilitate achievement of case goals and in doing so, decrease the length of time children spend in foster care.

Planning visits and making them meaningful for children and their parents are demanding and time-consuming tasks, but they are critically important to families and to case outcome. Our hope is that this resource will not only guide your work with families, but will also encourage you in your commitment to maintaining relationships between children and their parents.

A Guide to Practice begins by discussing the importance and purposes of visiting and by identifying the ways in which agency policies and placement practices encourage or constrain visiting. The second chapter introduces the concept of visiting as an essential component of agency service. It outlines the elements of the visiting plan, and recognizing that most children in care will return home, it describes the changes in visiting plans that should typically occur as the time for reunification nears. The following three chapters provide guidelines for considering factors related to children, their parents, and their substitute caregivers in developing visiting plans. These chapters focus on the individual assessments that must continually be made in each case in order to develop a sound visiting plan. The sixth chapter offers suggestions for preparing participants for visits and for evaluating and documenting visits. The book concludes with a discussion of the demands visiting imposes on workers and ways in which you can relieve some of the stress you encounter.

Throughout the book we have used the inclusive term "substitute caregiver." Children may be placed with a foster family, a relative, in a group home, or in a residential treatment facility. Although the process for planning visits and the role of the caregiver in visits may vary somewhat depending on the nature of the placement, the same guidelines for decision making concerning visits apply.

We have alternated the use of feminine and masculine pronouns for both children and parents throughout the book. The plural "parents" is used except when the discussion relates to an individual parent's visiting plan.

A Guide to Practice shares what we have learned from our research, from our own practice experiences, and from the experiences of our colleagues. Throughout the discussion we have asserted standards for practice, recognizing the realities that complicate your ability to achieve that standard in each case. Our discussion also reflects the literature related to visiting. We have not included, however, citations in the text to our research or to other literature regarding visiting. Several of these are listed in the bibliography.

We are grateful to the following persons for their assistance with this book. Several colleagues read and provided very useful comments on an earlier draft: Janet Deland, Jeanne Howard, Eve Krasinski, Carol Massat, Edie Olson, and Anita Osborn. Jane Winters cheerfully and ably typed the multiple drafts. We are particularly grateful to Carl Schoenberg of the Child Welfare League of America for his encouragement and for his wisdom and editorial skill.

1

Visiting in Context

Although visiting between children in placement and their families may often seem simply an agency requirement, visiting is critical to a child's well-being and to successful reunification of the family. Arranging visits and making them meaningful are two of the most important aspects of work with children in placement. This chapter discusses the importance and purposes of visiting, and it identifies the ways in which agency policies and resources support or constrain visiting. It provides information that you can use to encourage a child's parents to visit and to encourage a child's substitute caregivers to facilitate visiting. It also offers a background against which you can examine your own perceptions of visiting and your agency's policies concerning visiting.

Importance of Visiting

Available research suggests that visiting is important for two reasons. First, the psychological well-being and developmental progress of children in placement are enhanced by frequent contact with their parents. Second, children who are visited frequently by their parents are more likely to be returned to their parents' care than are children who are visited infrequently.

Perhaps more important than these research conclusions is the realization that children who are in placement are like all other children in being attached to their parents and to other members of their families. Children in placement miss their families when they are apart, and they miss their homes when they are away. Visiting, then, is important simply because it allows children to be with the people to whom they are attached, and if possible, to be in the homes they remember. Visiting becomes more than a casework tool; it is an expression of your caring for children. While visiting between children and their parents is the focus of most visit planning and of this book, visiting between children and other members of their families is also important. Siblings, grandparents, and other relatives are all part of the world from which children in placement have been uprooted.

1

Purposes of Visiting

The primary purpose of visiting is to allow children to preserve relationships with people who are important to them. This purpose supersedes all other purposes of visiting. It justifies visiting not only between parents and children, but also between siblings who are separated in placement, between children and members of their extended families, and in some cases, between children and foster parents who cared for them earlier. The child's need for continuity of relationships and the importance of visiting to continuity must be respected, even though visiting is also used for other purposes that are suggested below.

Although preservation of family relationships between children and parents and between siblings separated in placement is obviously essential to successful reunification, it is also important if the case goal is not reunification. In many cases children will and should remain attached to siblings and members of the extended family even when they will not return to parental care. These family members, like former substitute caregivers, may be important resources for children both while children are in care and when they reach adulthood. The relationships can only be maintained through frequent visiting.

While recognizing the value of visiting in and of itself, visiting can and should also be thought of as a planned intervention. This further justifies the development of visiting plans and the use of agency resources to support visiting. What are some of the purposes of visiting that make it an integral part of services to children in placement?

Reassurance

Visiting reassures children that they have not been abandoned, a common and psychologically damaging fear of children in placement. Visiting reassures parents that the agency wants the family to be unified again and is not trying to separate them from their children. Visiting also reassures children and other family members that everyone in the family is well, freeing them from unnecessary worry and releasing more energy to devote to developmental tasks or work on case goals.

Assessment

Visiting allows caseworkers to observe interactions between parents and children. This is a necessary prerequisite to developing the initial treatment plan, evaluating progress in meeting case goals, modifying the treatment plan, and determining if or when a child can return home. It also provides an opportunity for caseworkers to assess parental motivation and capacity. Are the parents willing to cooperate in establishing a visiting plan? Can they arrange their own transportation to the site of the visit or to pick up their child for the visit? Do they keep scheduled visit appointments? Can they plan appropriate activities for their children? Can they care for and protect their children during visits?

One qualification must be added. Although the answers to questions concerning motivation and capacity are important, perhaps essential, indicators of the probability of successful reunification, they must not be colored by barriers to visiting that might emanate from the agency. For example, some agency requirements regarding the parents' responsibilities in visiting may be impracticable, and if this is the case, a parent's failure to meet them must not be interpreted as lack of interest in the child.

Treatment

In many cases, treatment involves teaching skills to parents. During visits, caseworkers, homemakers, therapists, and children's foster parents can teach child care and demonstrate ways of setting and enforcing limits. The visit then becomes an integral and active part of treatment. Even when parenting skills are not being taught during the visits themselves, visits remain an important part of treatment. Visits provide an opportunity for parents to test and to improve the skills they might be learning in parenting classes or counseling sessions. Moreover, in cases where the relationship between parents and children is troubled, visits allow family members to develop better ways of interacting and communicating. And when parents and children are strongly attached, the prospect of more frequent and longer visits can be a powerful motivator to remain engaged in treatment.

Treatment necessarily involves confronting reality. Parents need to experience what child care and supervision really involve. Some parents need to decide whether they really want to be a parent. Some children need to confront the reality that their parents will never be able to care adequately for them; they may not be able to return home. Older children, if they are to return home, may have to assume more responsibility for their own care and protection. In some cases, parents need to acknowledge that their children are unwilling to return home and would undermine attempts to reunify the family. These realities can best be confronted—and perhaps can only be confronted—through visiting. Without visiting, abilities and desires are abstract and therefore unclear. In the absence of contact, it is easy for both parents and children to fantasize and to deny reality. Parents and children must experience being together to be able to determine for themselves if reunification is possible. Moreover, when reunification is not possible, it is easier for family members to accept that fact if it has been tested through extensive visiting.

Documentation

Recommendations either for return home or for termination of parental rights typically must be carefully justified. Documentation of not only the visiting plan, but also events that occur surrounding and during visits can support recommendations that you make. On the one hand, for example, if a parent who has been involved in visit planning and has agreed to a written visiting plan fails without just cause to visit, then there is reinforcement for termination of parental rights. On the other hand, if it can be shown that there was no evidence of abuse during visits that progressed from short visits in the office to visits overnight at home, then there is added support for return home.

Conditions That Optimize Visiting

If visiting is to occur frequently and be a significant component of service to families, certain conditions must be met. Some of these conditions are within your control; they concern your attitudes and the decisions you make. Others are not within your immediate control; these relate to your agency's policies and resources. An awareness of all these conditions, however, may help in understanding the limits of what can be achieved and may encourage you to seek changes in the policies and practices followed in your agency.

Caseworkers must be committed to visiting

Arranging and supporting visits are two of the most difficult and time-consuming aspects of caseworkers' work with children in placement. Visits can place enormous stress on you. You worry about children being physically or emotionally harmed during visits. You watch some children approach their parents during visits, only to be rejected or ignored. You try to comfort children when their parents fail to visit. You see the pain of good-byes and of parents' and children's attempts to reassure each other. You spend seemingly endless hours arranging a visit and coordinating transportation only to have a parent or foster parent cancel the visit at the last minute. Scheduling visits, especially for holidays and on children's birthdays, often seems to be a thankless task.

It is difficult for caseworkers to maintain their commitment to visiting in the face of the demands it imposes, but commitment is essential because the caseworker is pivotal in the case. Your commitment will influence parents, children, and other service providers. In many cases, your commitment to visiting may determine whether successful reunification occurs.

Caseworkers must have empathy for parents

It is easy to create barriers to visiting: to schedule visits at the office and only during regular business hours, to expect parents with no income or limited income to arrange their own transportation, and to view every missed visit as a sign of the parent's lack of caring or interest. In reality, visiting is extremely difficult for parents. It stirs their feelings of missing their children. It reminds them of their failures and inadequacies. Each visit tells parents that while they are not capable of caring for their children, someone else is. If the opportunity to visit is to be more than a test of parents' interest in their children, and perhaps an unreasonable test at that, visits must be planned with parents' needs and resources in mind.

Caregivers must be committed to visiting

Visiting does not depend only on the caseworker, the child, and the child's parents. Visiting also depends on the child's caregivers, who can either support or undermine the visiting plan.

Foster parents and child care workers play important roles in visiting. They can help prepare a child for a visit. They can comfort and reassure a child or respond in other ways that are helpful to a child following a visit. They can transport the child to and from visits. Foster parents can allow visits in their own homes and be actively involved in visits, modeling healthy parent-child interactions and teaching child care.

But foster parents and child care workers may be uncooperative in scheduling visits and reluctant to assist with transportation. They can show their dislike and distrust of a child's parents through words and actions. They can refuse to accept that a child's negative behaviors or withdrawal following visits indicate healthy attachment and distress over separation, and instead insist that visits occur less frequently in order to minimize the problems with which they must contend. Because of their ability to influence the child and the implementation of the agency plan, the willingness of substitute caregivers to facilitate visiting is critical.

Concerns about caregivers include not only your agency's foster parents or child care workers, but also the policies and practices of other agencies and placement facilities from which your agency may purchase services. In a survey of the policies of voluntary agencies, we found that some agencies had policies discouraging visits during the month immediately following placement. Some residential treatment facilities made the frequency and the site of visits depend on the child's behavior. Some agencies had policies prohibiting visits in the child's foster home. Policies of this kind may seem justified from the agencies' viewpoint, but they may result in strong resistance to plans you develop. In such instances, you may be required to enlist the support of your supervisor and your agency's administration to enforce your visiting plan.

Foster parents must not be overburdened

The difficulty of recruiting foster parents goes without saying, especially foster parents who are committed to reunification and to strengthening children's relationships with their families. It is easy to overuse such foster parents by asking that they take just one more child or that they take a child for whom they are reluctant to care, either because the child has special needs or because the child appears not to fit well with children already in the home. But by asking foster parents to care for too many children from different families or to care for too many children with special needs, we almost assure that visiting will become problematic, no matter how committed the foster parent is to visiting. Just as visiting places emotional demands on caseworkers and requires a significant amount of their time, it is emotionally demanding and time-consuming for foster parents. Foster parents simply do not have the emotional resources or the time to prepare many children for visits and respond helpfully to the children following visits. Similarly, if there are many children in the home, the foster parents cannot be as helpful in providing transportation for one child because they do not have the time, and they cannot be as flexible in scheduling. They must balance the need to care for the child who has the visit today with the need to care for other children in the home.

Children must be placed near their parents' homes

Federal policy requires that children be placed in the most family-like setting available and in close proximity to the parents' home, consistent with the best interests and special needs of the child. The extent to which this requirement is met has a direct impact on visiting.

Visits are easier to arrange when children are living in foster homes than when they are living in group care. In foster family care, you and the parent need only plan with the foster parents, taking into account only the child's and the foster parents' schedules. If children are in group care, however, visit planning must often take into account not only the child's needs and activities, but also those of the entire facility. Moreover, if the child is in group care, it may be more difficult to locate a visit site that offers privacy and an opportunity for natural interaction.

Even more important to visit planning than the type of placement is the nearness of the placement to the parents' home. The closer parents and children are geographically, the more frequently they can visit. This occurs for two reasons. First, it is reasonable to expect parents to visit more often and arrange their own transportation if they have less distance to travel. Second, if children and parents are located near each other, you and others do not need to spend as much time and money transporting.

Siblings must be placed together

It is critical that siblings be placed together whenever possible. Siblings who are separated in placement suffer greater loss and disruption of family life than do siblings who are not separated. They lose not only their parents, but also their brothers and sisters. Siblings who are placed together can offer each other support and reassurance. Moreover, if siblings are separated, reunification requires not only a reconstruction of parent-child relationships, but also reconstruction of sibling relationships.

The placement of siblings also influences visiting. If siblings are separated, visit planning becomes more complex. To illustrate, consider a case in which three children are placed in separate foster homes and in which the goal for all three children is return home. You must decide whether the parents are going to visit with all the children at once, or whether they are going to visit with the children individually. On the one hand, if parents are to visit all three children together, you must coordinate the parents' schedule with the schedules of the three children and their foster parents and perhaps with your schedule. The times when visits are convenient for all four households are likely to be few. On the other hand, if the parents visit the children individually, the time and cost spent in visiting becomes a significant consideration, not only for the parents, but also for you and for others providing supervision or transportation. Moreover, if the children are not together for visits with their parents, then you must arrange times for the children to visit each other.

Agency policy must require written plans for frequent visits

Policy requiring written plans for frequent visits appears to be an important prerequisite to frequent visiting and eventual reunification. Other researchers have found that the more frequently parents visit, the higher the probability of reunification. We have found (1) that case plans specify visiting in accord with agency policy, and (2) that parents visit in accord with case plans. If there is no schedule for visits, parents do not visit. But if there is a schedule, parents tend to keep it, especially if they were involved in making the schedule.

Policy articulates a preference as to what should occur. But more importantly, if policy specifies a given minimum visiting frequency, agency resources usually support the policy. Policy requiring, for example, a schedule specifying weekly visits will result in a schedule specifying weekly visits. In addition, policy gives caseworkers some authority or leverage in working with substitute caregivers who are reluctant to support frequent visits.

The importance of specific, written plans cannot be overstated. First, specific written visiting plans can prevent misunderstandings by clearly stating expectations and schedules. Second, specific and written plans, developed with the input of all parties involved in visiting, serve as contracts. Compliance with the contract can be used to support recommendations either to return children home or to terminate parental rights.

Agency resources must promote visiting

Agency resources have a profound effect on visiting. Visiting can occur only infrequently in the absence of resources to support it. What resources influence visiting?

Low and varied caseloads. Visiting is time-consuming for caseworkers. One visit, whether it is to be supervised or unsupervised, can easily take an entire afternoon. Moreover, if visiting is to be an integral part of services, you need time to plan the visit and its objectives, to prepare the parents and the child for it, and to discuss it with the parents and child after it has occurred. You also need time to discuss the visit with the child's foster parents after it has occurred, alerting them to any special needs the child might have, and noting any observations you would like them to make. You need time to document what occurred during the visit and how the participants reacted to it.

The demands visiting imposes on caseworkers' time must be considered in case assignments. If visiting is to occur frequently and to be used creatively, the number of cases in a caseload in which reunification is the goal or in which frequent visiting is to be encouraged for other reasons must be low. The higher the caseload, and the greater the number of cases in which reunification is the goal, the less frequent the visiting is likely to be. When caseloads are high, visiting is also less likely to be a meaningful part of the treatment plan.

Placement resources. The frequency of visiting depends on the geographic distance between the parents and the child, the extent to which siblings are separated, and the commitment and resources of caregivers. All of these factors relate to the quantity and quality of placement resources available to the agency. Visiting can occur frequently and be used creatively in concert with case goals only when the agency has placement resources that allow children to be placed together near their parents and with caregivers who are committed to visiting.

Flexible hours. Visits, if they are to meet the needs of parents and children, often should not occur during the standard working hours of nine to five or eight to four. Instead, they should occur on weekends, in the evenings, and over holidays. Visiting will be supported by agency policy allowing flextime or compensation for work outside of normal business hours. Similarly, visiting will be supported if the agency has regular scheduled working hours at times convenient for parents, for example, evening and weekend hours.

Private and comfortable visiting rooms. Visits often cannot or should not occur in the parents' home primarily because of concerns over the child's safety. At times visiting in the foster home may not be advisable. However, visits should be held at a site that allows for privacy and natural interaction. In order to use visits at least in part for assessment, they need to be held where the visit can be unobtrusively observed. For these reasons, the various purposes of visiting can best be achieved if the agency has well-equipped, comfortable visiting rooms with one-way mirrors.

Volunteers and others to assist with visiting. Volunteers, homemakers, therapists, and other professionals can be very helpful in visiting, easing the demands placed on caseworkers. Volunteers and others can transport children and parents to visits and, in some instances, supervise visits. Simply put, agencies with committed volunteers can offer more visiting than agencies without volunteers, and agencies who can pay staff members other than caseworkers to assist with visiting can schedule more frequent visits.

Financial assistance for parents. An aspect of visiting that is often overlooked is its cost to parents. If a visit is not at their home, the parents may have to pay for transportation and for the care of children who are at home. If the visit is at their home, the parents need to buy extra food and pay other costs of caring for the child. Although none of these costs are extreme, they can be significant to a parent on a very low income or no income at all, as is the case with a parent whose sole source of income was AFDC before the child's placement. If the agency is to expect or encourage frequent visits or extended home visits, it must have some way to assist parents with the costs of visiting.

2

Visiting as a Component of the Service Plan

Visiting does not occur at the whim of parents and caseworkers, independent of case goals and agency services. Visiting is a planned intervention, and the visiting plan is an essential component of the service plan. The visiting plan is based in part on the permanency goal for the child, and therefore should help achieve the goal and reflect progress toward it.

Because most children in placement should and will return home, visiting in most cases will be used to support the goal of reunification. But even when return home is not the goal, visiting should usually continue to play a role in the service plan.

Service and Visit Planning Assumptions

The discussion of service and visit planning in this chapter is premised on several assumptions.

The agency is obligated to develop plans

Service and visit planning is the responsibility of the agency, not the parent. Consistent with federal law and law in most states, the agency is obligated to take the initiative in developing service plans for families with children in placement. As part of this plan, the agency must develop a plan that allows children to have frequent contact with their parents, with siblings who may be placed elsewhere, and with other persons who cared for the children prior to placement. The service and visiting plans should be reviewed at least every six months.

Planning must involve parents, children, and others

Client involvement in service planning is a time-honored principle that is often set aside, especially when clients are unresponsive or hostile. But if they are to be expected to comply with service and visiting plans, parents

11

must be involved in developing the plans. Moreover, when change depends not only on the parents, but also on the child, as is the case with older children, the child must also be involved. Children, especially adolescents, can easily subvert the best-laid plans. Their cooperation is essential.

Gathering and assessing the information needed to develop sound visiting plans requires collaboration with others. Visit plans that best support the service plan reflect accurate, current information from service providers concerning the progress of parents. The person supervising visits has valuable information regarding parent-child interactions. Others, including substitute caregivers and children's teachers, may also have pertinent information. Case conferences are usually an efficient and effective way to pool and assess information for planning.

No one is free from biases. All of us welcome support when making difficult decisions. Therefore, planning visits, as with other decision making in cases, is strengthened by the review of supervisors and peers. Case conferences and team decision making generate creative options, decrease the influence of personal bias on case decisions, and reduce the stresses associated with planning visits and services.

The plan must be known to all essential persons

All persons involved in service provision and in visiting must be familiar with the service and visiting plans. When everyone essential to the success of a plan is aware of it, individuals are less likely to be working at cross-purposes and the probability of achieving case goals is increased.

It is therefore important that the original plan be in writing and that as the visiting plan is changed, any changes be specified in writing and a copy given to everyone who is involved in carrying out the plan. It is also important that, consistent with applicable federal and state laws, parents be informed that they have a right to appeal changes in the visiting plan.

There is a preferred visiting plan

There is a preferred visiting plan in every case that will best meet individual children's and parents' needs and closely parallel the service plan. You may respond to this statement by saying, "But that's the ideal...." Yes, it is the ideal. Reaching for the ideal in a plan does not deny the realities that may affect implementation; but assuming that the preferred or ideal plan can never be implemented guarantees that we will fall short of our standard. Determining the preferred plan encourages caseworkers, substitute caregivers, and other service providers to identify and try to eliminate obstacles to implementation. Moreover, developing a preferred plan can encourage practice that is less crisis oriented.

Developing visiting plans is complicated

Developing sound visiting plans is not easy. In fact, caseworkers who find visit planning easy or clear-cut are likely to be overlooking something. This complex process requires that changing (yet current) information be gathered continually from several sources. For example, you need to know the current schedules of the child, the parents, the caregivers, and the persons transporting others to or supervising visits. Developing plans also requires knowledge about human development, behavior, and change; and skill in making professional judgements, including the assessment of risk and of family progress.

The development of visiting plans is complicated by needing to anticipate and plan for the unpredictable. When people are under stress, their feelings are intense and their behaviors are often impulsive. Although human behavior is never fully predictable, you must project the answers to questions such as: "Might the child be harmed or abducted during the visit?" "Will the parent arrive for the visit as agreed to in the plan?"

Conflicts in determining the preferred plan are inevitable

The needs, requests, and expectations of those affected by the visiting plan often conflict, suggesting different perceptions of the preferred visiting plan. For example, a parent's right to frequent and increasingly unrestricted contact may conflict with the child's expressed preference. Parents' and foster parents' preferences concerning visit frequency or other arrangements may conflict. These conflicts are inevitable, but they must and can be resolved. The following considerations guide the resolution of such conflicts:

1. Visit planning conflicts involving realistic concerns for a child's safety and security should be resolved through weighing this concern more heavily than any other.

2. When the family members' right to contact conflicts with the needs or preferences of substitute caregivers or service providers, the conflict should be resolved in a way that protects and assures the family members' right to contact.

3. When visit plan options offer varying degrees of support to the service plan, for example, with regard to visit length or visit site, weight should be given to the plan that best supports the

service plan, even when that plan is less convenient or requires additional agency resources.

4. When expectations as to who should be included in visits differ, the child's and the parents' preferences should be given priority over those of substitute caregivers or extended family members.

5. When limited resources create a conflict with any aspect of the preferred visiting plan, every effort should be made to develop or access resources in order to carry out the preferred plan.

The plan must reflect careful risk assessment

Removal of most children from their own homes is designed to prevent harm. Therefore, most decisions concerning parent-child contact involve assessment of risk to the child. It must be emphasized that with regard to visit planning, risk assessment must be current and case-specific. Depending on the family's service use and current situation, risk to a child may increase or decrease within a brief period of time.

The parents' ability and willingness to appropriately care for, relate to, and protect the child at any point in time affects all aspects of the visit arrangements. Continual assessment of parental behaviors and of abilities that relate to the reason for placement and to risk to the child is therefore essential. Several frameworks for risk assessment are available and are useful in risk assessment as it relates to visit planning.*

Since risk assessment is case-specific, you cannot automatically generalize from one case to another. The fact that a child in one case was harmed in a particular visiting situation does not mean that all children in your caseload visiting in that situation are vulnerable.

A critical aspect of risk assessment is determining whether a child is being harmed during visits. Many children present behaviors following visits that are troublesome and distressing to substitute caregivers. It is not uncommon, for example, for children to be enuretic for several nights following a visit, to withdraw to their rooms immediately upon returning from a visit, to reject caregivers, to be argumentative, or to be less well

---

*   Magura, Stephen; Moses, Beth Silverman; and Jones, Mary Ann. *Assessing Risk and Measuring Change in Families: The Family Risk Scales*. Washington, DC: Child Welfare League of America, 1987.
    Snyder, Eunice, and Ramo, Keetjie. *Deciding To Place or Not To Place*. Cheney, WA: School of Social Work and Human Services, Eastern Washington University, 1983.

behaved. Behaviors such as these are often interpreted by caregivers and caseworkers as indicators that the children were harmed, leading almost always to efforts to decrease the frequency and length of visits or to hold visits at a site other than a child's home.

But do these behaviors necessarily indicate that the children are being harmed? The answer in the vast majority of cases is no. Visiting disrupts a child's routine, can be physically tiring, and inevitably stirs deep feelings in a child, feelings that most children have difficulty verbalizing. The troubled behavior following visits is typically the result of fatigue and the disruption of routine and reflects the child's attachment to parents and the pain of separation.

There are times, however, when the behaviors just discussed and other behaviors do indicate that the children are being harmed. Indications of distress can be distinguished from harm only by observing the children and parents and by talking with the children. Does the child visibly cringe at a parent's touch? Does the child continue to cling to you well into the visit rather than go to a parent? Is there physical evidence of abuse? Do the behaviors described above persist for days after the visit and interfere with the child's functioning in many areas? What does the child say when asked to describe the visit?

If it appears that the child is reacting to the pain of separation, you might consider increasing the frequency of visits. Frequent visits more easily become a part of a child's routine and are therefore less disruptive. More frequent visits can ease the pain of each good-bye. If there is evidence of harm during unsupervised visits, however, the plan must be changed to allow only closely supervised visits, and an evaluation must be completed regarding the impact of visiting on the child.

Visiting should never be used as a reward or as a punishment

Visiting arrangements directly depend on assessment of the parents' ability and of the risk to the child. As parents can assume greater responsibility for child care and supervision, visits are planned more often, for longer periods, more frequently in the parents' home, and with fewer restrictions. Arrangements, therefore, are a logical consequence of the assessment of parenting behaviors and the family situation, not a reward.

The distinction between perceiving changes in visiting arrangements as a logical consequence or as a reward is quite important. When you view changes in visiting as directly related to assessment of changes in families, visiting arrangements can be developed openly and as part of the agency's service plan. When caseworkers or other service providers (for example, treatment facilities) use visits to reward behaviors of parents or children, such as keeping appointments, they misuse the authority inherent in their position. Further, family members may assume that compliance in service use, rather than change in behavior, is all they need to demonstrate. Equating progress solely with service use leads to false assumptions of change by caseworkers that may ultimately endanger the child and undermine achievement of case goals.

When parents do not make the personal or situational changes required to assure the safety of children, maintaining a more restrictive visiting plan is not a punishment, it is a means of child protection. Rather than promising increased visiting as a leverage or an incentive, you should deal directly with the lack of progress. Are services inappropriate or ineffective? Are there obstacles to service use? Are the parents ambivalent about contact with their child or about family reunification?

When visit arrangements are viewed by the caseworker and the family as rewards or punishments for either parents or children, the caseworker's authority over plan changes is magnified. Family members' fears of the misuse of this authority, ever present, are likely to be heightened and become an obstacle in the client-caseworker relationship. Visit changes may then easily be perceived as (and may be) capricious or punitive. You can help parents and children understand that visits are not used as rewards or punishments by acknowledging in your initial discussion with them that many families fear that visiting may be used in this way. Describe the relationship between visiting arrangements and the assessment of change in families. Then, throughout the placement, openly discuss the reasons for all visiting decisions.

Children and parents have a right to see each other. That right should be restricted only when there is a danger to the child. As the danger decreases or increases, so does the restriction. It has nothing to do with reward and punishment.

Elements of the Visiting Plan

The visiting plan should specify the following elements: (1) frequency, site and length of scheduled visits; (2) if and how visits are to be supervised; (3) who is to participate in the visits; (4) tasks to be accomplished during visits; and (5) agency and parental responsibilities attendant to visits.

Each of these elements is discussed below. As you read, you should keep in mind that none of these elements remains static during the course of a child's placement. Instead, as we will discuss later, predictable changes should occur as the time for reunification nears or as the agency works to achieve an alternative permanency goal. In addition, changes that cannot be predicted may be necessary when crises occur, such as a parent's or a child's hospitalization or a death in the child's family.

Frequency

Visit frequency includes both how quickly after placement the first visit occurs and how often visiting occurs throughout the placement. We believe that the first visit should occur within 48 hours of the placement to reassure children that their parents have not abandoned them. Many states require that following the initial visit, visits be scheduled at least once a week. This minimum frequency is particularly important for young children who experience even seven days as an eternity. Weekly visits, however, should be viewed as the base frequency rather than the standard. As the time for reunification nears, visits should occur more often than once a week.

Length

Visit length may range from an hour to several days. As discussed later, visit length must provide sufficient time for natural interaction and for completion of activities related to the service plan.

Location

The locations of visits should (1) be only as restrictive as is necessary to assure the child's safety; (2) allow for privacy and for natural interaction; and (3) whenever possible be in the parents' home. The visit site should reflect the purpose of the visit and be identified in the visit plan.

Supervision

Visits in some cases may need to be supervised in order to protect children, assess and document interaction, or teach parents. Visits may be supervised by different persons at different times depending on the purpose of the supervision. The purpose of supervision and the identity of the persons supervising (i.e., caseworker, foster parent, home educator, visiting nurse, or volunteer) should be included in the visiting plan.

Participants

The visiting plans should specify who may or may not visit and by what process the agency will consider exceptions. Most children in placement have a significant relationship with persons other than their parents—grandparents, friends of their parents, previous substitute caregivers, or others. When this is the case, these persons should be included in at least some visits if the child requests it and if their presence does not endanger the child or subvert achievement of case goals.

Supportive services

Services to facilitate visiting are often necessary and should be spelled out in the visiting plan. Who will transport the child? Are the parents responsible for their transportation? Will any financial assistance be provided to the parents? Will the agency provide child care for children who are living at home?

Activities

Parents may be expected to perform specific tasks related to child care during visits. These activities should be appropriate to the developmental age of the child and facilitate natural interaction between parent and child. Examples of appropriate visiting activities include accompanying the child to medical and dental appointments, shopping for clothes, and attending school conferences and open houses. When parents are expected to perform certain tasks, this should be clearly stated in the plan.

Conditions

In individual cases, parents may be required to meet conditions related to visits. For example, a parent may be required to call in advance to confirm his or her intention to keep a visit appointment, to remain sober throughout the visit, to refrain from promising at each visit to take the child home at the end of the visit, to refrain from using physical discipline, or to refrain from bringing other persons to the visit without advance agency approval. Any such conditions must be specified in the case plan.

Placement Phases

Service to most children in placement follows a rather predictable sequence. Immediately following placement, the emphasis is on assessment, goal setting, and service planning. Following this initial phase, which usually lasts about 30 days, the agency and family work together to make the changes necessary for the agency to recommend that the child return home. We have termed this phase the central phase. Activity during this phase will determine the outcome of service. This phase will often extend over several months or even years. Reunification is the final placement phase in the typical case, beginning when the decision is made to return a child to parental custody and when service providers and family members make specific plans for return. This phase of placement ends when parents assume full-time care and custody, with the agency's, and if necessary, the court's approval. The emphasis in this phase is on facilitating a smooth transition from placement to home and determining what services will be provided after the child has returned home. In cases when the child cannot return home, the central phase is followed by a reassessment phase during which alternate case goals are established.

Visiting Phases

Predictable changes in the visiting plan correspond to each placement phase. These changes concern both visit purposes and arrangements.

Changing purposes of visiting

As discussed in chapter 1, visiting has many purposes. Visiting can provide an opportunity for workers to:

assess the parent-child relationship;

assess the parents' ability to adequately and appropriately care for and relate to the child;

help the parents develop appropriate parenting behaviors;

help the child interact with the parents;

identify and resolve problems before the child returns home;

evaluate the family's progress toward targeted changes;

assess the feasibility and timing of the child's return home; and

facilitate the child's transition to the parents' home.

Although each purpose may apply to some extent throughout all the phases of placement, each is not of equal importance during each phase. For example, visiting is used primarily for assessment during the initial phase. While assessment continues throughout placement, visiting is used less for assessment and more for teaching and for problem identification and resolution during the central phase. Visiting is used during the reunification phase primarily to ease the transition from placement to home and to determine what services will be needed to support the family following reunification. As you use visiting for specific casework objectives, however, you should keep in mind that when the goal is reunification, the underlying and most important purpose of visiting through all phases of placement is always to maintain parent-child attachment.

Changing visit arrangements

You should develop the initial visiting plan with the expectation that changes will be made often, but planfully. When the case goal is return home and the family progresses toward that goal, visit arrangement changes should follow a planned and predictable sequence. Over time, visits will be more frequent and occur more often in the child's own home. They will be longer and less supervised. In short, as reunification nears, the primary responsibility for the child's care and protection during visits shifts from the agency to the parents.

Visiting plans during the initial assessment phase

A child's placement is almost always a result of a professional judgment that even with the use of home-based services, a child is in danger if he or she remains at home. Occasionally placement occurs because a parent is hospitalized or incarcerated. Regardless of the reason for placement, the extent to which the agency controls visiting arrangements and supervises visits throughout the placement should depend on the parents' ability at any point in time to care for the child appropriately and the child's level of comfort with the parents.

Immediately following placement, the child and parents are often uncomfortable with each other. This is a typical reaction to placement. In their frustration and anger about the child's placement, parents may blame the child for the placement. Sometimes parents pressure their children to recant their allegations of maltreatment. If the child had to be placed before home-based services could be provided, there may be little information available about the family. If placement is the result of a parent's or child's treatment needs or a parent's incarceration, confusion may exist about the duration and probable outcome of the placement. Regardless of the circumstances, placement is usually a devastating event for both parents and children, and visiting initially is awkward.

During the first month following placement, you therefore will typically need to supervise visits and to carefully control visit location, length, and participants. By doing so you can ease the awkwardness of visits by facilitating interaction between parents and children. You can protect the child as needed. You can gather important information about the parent-child relationship and patterns of interaction. But whatever the reason for your presence during visits, you should remember that the primary purpose of visiting is to maintain the relationship between parent and child. Unless the child would be endangered, allow some time for the parent and child to be alone.

The initial visits, even when closely supervised, should be conducted in the most natural setting possible—the child's home, the foster home, or a comfortable visiting room. Natural interaction is simply impossible in a room with a desk and four chairs; and observation under such circumstances will be of limited usefulness.

Visiting plans during the central phase

As the family's service needs are identified and the family begins to make the changes necessary for the child's return home, the case enters the central phase. Visit arrangements continue to reflect the agency's responsibility to assure the child's safety and security, but they also will be used to achieve case goals. Visits provide a crucial opportunity for parents and children to learn and practice new skills and patterns of behavior together. Visits also allow for further identification and resolution of family problems. From the vantage point of both the agency and the family, visiting during the central phase provides experiences and information necessary for assessing the feasibility and timing of the child's return home.

One could think of visits during the central phase as an "internship" in family functioning. Family members try to apply what they have learned in parent education classes, counseling, or work with the agency home educator or public health nurse. As they succeed within a particular visiting arrangement, changes in the arrangement should be made to allow for further progression toward the child's return home. When families do not succeed, you have to assess whether changes in the visiting arrangements or in service provision could provide greater support for success. For example, perhaps the parents need someone present during visits to give immediate suggestions and feedback regarding their care of the children.

The visit plan during the central phase should specify that visits will incrementally occur more often and be longer. To illustrate, a young mother whose infant was placed for failure to thrive visited in the foster home three mornings a week for two hours each morning, helping with feeding and bathing. For three weeks the mother kept the visiting schedule, worked at caring for her child, and responded better to the child's needs. The visit plan was then changed to visits for the entire morning on two of the three days a week with less involvement of the foster mother, allowing the mother greater responsibility for the child's care for a longer period, including two feedings. After three weeks with longer visits, an additional morning-long visit was to be scheduled weekly, but in the mother's own home with supervision provided by an agency homemaker. These incremental steps reflected the agency's expectation that the mother assume more responsibility for her child's care as quickly as she was able, but improved the likelihood of success with each step by assuring that her child would be adequately cared for and safe during the process.

As illustrated in this example, agency supervision should diminish as responsibility is gradually shifted to the parents. In an office visit, for instance, shifting might involve initially participating in the visit and intervening when indicated; to sitting in the room listening, but focusing on paperwork; to occasionally observing through a one-way mirror; to being available in one's office should the parents or child request assistance. Eventually, the visits might take place in public away from the office, in the child's foster home, or in the child's own home, again with decreasing degrees of monitoring. At a certain point, nonfamily members, such as the parents' and child's friends, may be included in the visits. Increased flexibility concerning both visit location and participants allows for more natural interaction. The family and child are thus supported in moving toward reunification.

Orchestrating a family's successful progression through the sequence of changes in arrangements requires making informed judgments about the child's safety, constant integrating of the visit plan with other aspects of the family's service plan, and time. Time must be invested in preparing the child, the parents, and the substitute caregivers for the visit, and in coordinating and careful monitoring of visit arrangements. Guidelines for assisting families through this sequence are provided in the following chapters.

Two changes that occur during the central phase are critical with regard to the shift from agency to parental responsibility: the point at which visits are no longer supervised, and the point at which the child stays overnight in the parents' home. Both require particular attention to risk assessment, and to support for the parents, child, and the child's substitute caregivers—topics that will be discussed in chapters that follow. In some agencies, these changes require supervisory or court review and approval.

The importance of the shift from agency to parental responsibility cannot be overstated. A judgment that reunification planning can proceed is premature until the family has had the opportunity to carry full child care responsibilities unsupervised and overnight, and until service providers and the family determine that the child is safe in those situations.

Visiting plans during the reunification phase

The reunification phase of the placement is marked by a shift in service planning. Rather than assessing the feasibility of returning home, emphasis is placed on assuring a smooth transition from placement to family home, on determining when parents can assume full-time custody, and on identifying services to support the family following reunification. Successful reunification may be doomed if it occurs precipitously, and if the family does not have opportunities to identify and resolve problems before the child returns home. The family must be able to experience gradually the changes that occur in the family system as the child is home for longer visits and parents assume greater responsibility for the child's care.

The use of visiting to facilitate successful reunification is illustrated in the following case. Reunification was planned for two children in January. During September, the children had visits at home that began after school on Friday and ended late Saturday afternoon, according to plan. In mid-October, a school holiday provided the opportunity for a four-day visit. The Friday afternoon through Saturday afternoon visits then continued until Thanksgiving, when the plan called for the children to live at home during the week and at the foster home on the weekends. This arrangement enabled the parents to readjust to the responsibility for daily care and to getting the children to school while providing for respite during the transition. This continued for the four weeks between Thanksgiving and mid-December, when the children's school holiday began. At this point, the plan provided for an extended visit at home, with the assumption that if the transition continued to go well, the children would then remain full-time in their parents' care. In early January, the agency and family members agreed that return home was a viable plan. The court approved return to the parents' custody full-time, with agency supervision.

Clearly, a visiting plan of this nature requires the commitment of the agency and the substitute caregivers to a transition period that eases the major changes families must cope with at reunification. Visits during this period must provide maximum opportunity for parent-child contact; for parental responsibility for the child, particularly in areas where breakdown previously occurred; and for evaluation of remaining stress points. These arrangements are successful if they, on the one hand, facilitate the child's successful move home, or, on the other hand, forestall premature reunification by identifying important unresolved problems.

In many cases where more than one child in a family is in placement, not all children will return home at the same time. Visit planning must be carefully individualized with particular attention to the needs of each child.

Visiting plans when reunification is not the goal

Visiting does not end when it is determined that reunification is not the goal. First, it must be remembered that unless parental rights are terminated or visits are prohibited by court order, parents and children have the right to visit. An agency decision against reunification in and of itself does not abrogate this right. And even if parental rights are terminated, visiting may take place during the appeals process. Second, visiting continues to play a vital role in the service plan, a role that in some cases is time-limited and that in others will continue indefinitely.

Through visiting, you can assist the family members, particularly the child, in dealing with the planned change in their relationship whether or not there is a plan for continuing contact in the future. In most instances, the change in case goal reflects the parents' unwillingness or inability to make the changes necessary for the child to return home. Children must be helped to understand why they cannot return home, the nature of the relationship they will have with their parents in the future, and the alternate permanency plan. They must be helped to work through their feelings about this reality, and visiting is an important part of this process.

When the goal is independent living or long-term placement, and both the child and the parents are interested in maintaining contact, the service plan and visiting plans should provide for continuing contact unless there is compelling justification to the contrary. Continuing contact can help the child develop self-esteem and a positive identity, and it can maintain family relationships that may endure and support the child when agency service ends.

In instances where all contact will be disconnected because of termination of parental rights or a court order prohibiting contact, you should consider planning a visit and/or other contacts, such as letters, for good-byes, and rituals related to good-byes, such as picture taking. Often, because of your own discomfort or concern to protect a child, you may interpret children's seeming lack of interest in seeing their parents as an indication that they have forgotten them or do not want contact. This interpretation is usually incorrect. In fact, many children in placement need permission to openly show and talk about their feelings. Planning a good-bye visit gives this permission. The visits themselves can help family members accept the reality of changed or ending relationships, contributing vitally to the grieving and healing process for both children and parents.

Case-Specific Considerations

This chapter has discussed the assumptions that undergird service and visit planning, the phases of service through which children in placement typically pass, and the visiting plans that correspond to these phases of placement. This discussion might have seemed to suggest that all you need to know to develop the visiting plan is the case goal and the phase of placement. As you know from experience, this is far from true. Visiting plans depend not only on the case goal and phase of placement but also on a variety of factors unique to each case that relate primarily to each child's characteristics and needs, to each parent's functioning, and to family relationships. Visiting plans for children are also affected by their substitute caregiver's capacity and willingness to be involved in various aspects of visiting.

Throughout a placement, case-specific information concerning the child, the child's parents, and the child's substitute caregivers shapes the visiting plan. None of the information gathered stands alone. For example, both the child's needs and parents' functioning must not only be assessed, but also examined in terms of the current fit between them. Ways in which case-specific information regarding the child, the parents, family relationships, and the substitute caregivers shape the plan are identified in the next three chapters.

3

Case Specific Considerations: The Children

The preferred visiting plan depends in part on the child's age, requests regarding visits, reactions to visits, developmental and therapeutic needs, and schedule.

Children's Chronological and Developmental Age

Each child's actual age and developmental age may differ. Many children in foster family and group placements do not function at the developmental levels their ages would suggest. Because of the unique abilities and needs of each child, it is not possible to provide hard-and-fast age-related guidelines for visiting. Some generalizations, however, are possible. For example, no matter what the developmental age, infants and toddlers are unable to provide self-care and supervision, and they cannot sustain the memory of their parents without very frequent contact. Therefore, the child's actual and developmental ages suggest answers to the following questions that must be raised in each case in planning visits.

How frequently does this child need to have parental contact?

Understanding the child's age-related sense of time helps you anticipate how the child will experience the absence of parents between each visit and to plan visit frequency accordingly. The child's sense of time has been described by well-known theorists as "the interval before a leave-taking will be experienced as a permanent loss, accompanied by feelings of helplessness and profound deprivation."* From an adult perspective, one week without parent-child contact goes quickly. For the infant or toddler, seven days are an eternity. Children's experiences of separation are

---

* Goldstein, Joseph; Freud, Anna; and Solnit, Albert. *Beyond the Best Interests of the Child*. New York: The Free Press, 1973, p. 42.

shaped by their ability to retain the memory or image of their absent parents. As memory develops with age, children can recall that their parents returned following previous separations. This capacity increases children's ability to understand and tolerate their parents' leaving and returning.

The child's age and sense of time, therefore, are primary considerations in planning frequency of visits. As noted earlier, visits should occur at least weekly. For infants, toddlers, and preschoolers, contact more often than weekly is warranted from the beginning of placement to decrease the child's sense of abandonment, to protect the parent-child attachment, and to assist the child in moving from one home to another.

What is the child's capacity for self-care?

In planning visit length, supervision, and location, you must consider the child's capacity for self-care. This capacity is related in large part to developmental age, but it also relates to special needs of the child. The degree of this capacity depends on the reason for placement and the parents' functioning at any point in time. To illustrate, school-age children who can follow instructions, fix sandwiches, and dress without help will be at less risk during lengthy unsupervised visits at home with a parent who has been neglectful than an infant or toddler will be. Similarly, an eight-year-old whose development has progressed age-appropriately will be at less risk than an eight-year-old who is developmentally delayed or whose special needs complicate self-care.

How vulnerable is this child to potentially harmful situations?

Actual and developmental ages similarly suggest a child's ability to recognize a potentially volatile or dangerous situation, leave the situation, and/or call for help, all of which influence the choices for supervision, duration, and location of visits. Because some children may not be willing to ask for help during a visit when doing so means exposing their parents' problematic behaviors, the assessment of the child's vulnerability must address this factor as well as the child's age and capacity.

The ability of children to protect themselves is particularly important during the central and reunification phases as families show progress and unsupervised home visits are being considered. For example, children of parents who have demonstrated progress in their recovery from substance abuse, in managing anger, or in complying with treatment for mental illness may differ in their ability to recognize and cope with potentially harmful situations. If a parent who is a recovering alcoholic begins to drink during an unsupervised visit, a child even as young as six or seven may be able to call a neighbor, the worker, substitute caregiver, or police for help in getting away from the situation. Younger or less capable children visiting with the same parent during the same placement phase will need more protection during visits, and unsupervised home visits may be delayed until the parent demonstrates more appropriate behavior.

How able is this child to structure his or her own activities?

Children's ages, as well as their temperaments, influence what they can manage or tolerate in visits. Does a child become bored and fussy easily? Is a child unable to entertain herself for a period of time while her mother cares for younger siblings? If so, it might be useful to have someone present during visits—particularly those that occur early in the placement—to help parents attend to the child. In addition, it is useful to identify activities that the child and parent enjoyed before placement and plan visits to include them. Walks, trips to park playgrounds, playing games, and playing with dolls or other toys are all appropriate visit activities that can extend the interaction between children and parents.

Children's Requests

Children indicate preferences about visit arrangements both directly ("Please stay with me while I'm with my dad") and indirectly ("You haven't sat in on my visits with dad in a while"). However expressed, you should try to determine what is behind a child's request before making or changing visit arrangements. The following example illustrates the importance of understanding what the child's concerns or interests are.

> Sara, an eight-year-old, asked her caseworker if it would be all right for her to visit with her family less often. When her worker explored what prompted this request, it was clear that Sara actually looked forward to her visits and enjoyed being with both of her parents. Further exploration revealed that Sara had overheard her foster parents discussing their unhappiness with the frequency of visits. She was afraid that they were angry with her for wanting to see her parents and worried that they were going to ask that she be moved.

In this instance, intervention with the foster parents, not a change in visit frequency, was indicated. In contrast, in exploring a similar request you might find that a child prefers less frequent visits because he is frightened. A decrease in visit frequency, however, may still be inappro-

priate. Fears might better be allayed by helping his parents understand how
their behavior threatens him, by more closely supervising the visits, or by
changing the location of the visits.

As you prepare children for visits and observe their reactions after
visits, you must not only identify but also try to understand their requests
and reactions. Your understanding then helps you decide what response
is appropriate.

Children's Reactions to Visits

Visits seem to present a Catch-22 for children. When children aren't
visited, they feel abandoned and become estranged from their families. But
when children are visited, they often experience distress in anticipation of
the visit, during the visit, in separating from their parents as the visit ends,
and during the separation immediately following the visit. Those providing
children's daily care—foster parents and child care workers—are often
asked to record and report children's reactions. When the reactions present
their caregivers with management problems, such as disobedience, their
caregivers may demand less frequent or shorter visits. You may also directly
observe a child's distress and automatically conclude that less contact with
the parent would be helpful. Before determining whether, or in what ways,
the plan should be altered, however, each of the following four questions
should be answered.

Is the reaction normal given the stresses of placement?

As discussed earlier, many children experience distress related to the
end of each visit and to the separation following visits. An increase in
frequency and/or duration of visits may relieve this distress and should be
considered. More frequent and longer visits increase the ability of most
children to cope with the separation and to adjust to placement. In addition,
telephone calls and letters between visits can ease the pain of separation.

Does the reaction reflect distress related to conflicting loyalties?

Placement inevitably places children in a double bind. They are
expected to fit in with foster family or group placement, while simultane-
ously maintaining their identification with their family. When substitute
caregivers support visits and accept children's affection for and identification with their families, children are freer to talk about and examine their
intense, often ambivalent, feelings about family, visiting, and return home.

Children who are either subtly or openly encouraged to shift their loyalty and their primary affections to the substitute caregivers are in a no-win position. They feel guilty and confused. They may act as if they prefer not to be with their parents to avoid displeasing the substitute caregivers with whom, after all, they spend most of their time. They are likely to repress or "stuff" their reactions, and the result may be problematic behavior, withdrawal, or depression.

Children are also sometimes confronted by their parents' demand that they not cooperate with their foster parents or child care workers: "They're not your parents, you don't have to obey them." This, too, places children in a no-win position.

When children's reactions to visits reflect even in part the lack of their substitute caregivers' support for their relationship with their families, immediate intervention is necessary. Intervention typically involves counseling with children and substitute caregivers to help them deal with the difficult situation the placement has created. If substitute caregivers are unable to support visiting, even after your interventions, a move may be necessary. Similarly, where parents undercut the child's efforts to adjust to the placement, intervention with the child and the parents is indicated.

Does the reaction reveal problems in the visiting situation?

When children are distressed by the visiting situation, changes in the visit arrangements and/or other interventions may be indicated. In many instances, families need continual assistance in planning and structuring visits. Parents often need your repeated help in thinking through what activities are age-appropriate, of interest to the child, and suited to the length and location of the visit. Parents sometimes need help in planning reasonably healthy snacks or meals. Repeated open discussion of appropriate visit rules and discipline helps decrease the discomfort for the child created by inconsistency between family and placement expectations.

Does the reaction indicate problems in the parent-child relationship?

When problems in the parent-child relationship contribute to the child's reaction to visits, additional diagnostic and therapeutic work is most likely indicated for the parents, child, and/or parents and child together. Problems of this nature are typically indicated by the intensity and persistence of the child's reaction. For example:

Granger, age ten, who had been physically abused by his father, had weekly supervised visits with him in an agency visiting room.

Not only was the child's extreme discomfort with his father obvious during the visits, but Granger also developed a pattern of problematic behaviors in school on visit day only. He had been warned by his teacher that when he misbehaved, he would have to stay after school. Thus, his misbehavior was resulting in his being late for, or missing, visits.

When relationship problems appear to be harmful to the children, the agency should document the behaviors of the parents and the reactions of the children and consider seeking a court-ordered change in the visit arrangements. The burden of demonstrating the association between the parents' behaviors, the children's reactions, and harm to the children typically falls on the agency. Therefore, consistent specific documentation of directly observed interactions is necessary. Whenever visits are considered harmful, agency supervision for the purposes of child protection, assessment, and documentation is essential.

Children's Developmental Tasks

Children who are in placement are often thought of as children in placement rather than as children. Their developmental tasks (which may or may not coincide with their actual age) are often overlooked as intervention focuses on improvement of their parents' functioning. In reality, children who are in placement, like all children, are growing physically, emotionally, socially, and intellectually and need the help of their parents, as well as their substitute caregivers, to accomplish developmental tasks.

The child's current developmental tasks should be considered in planning visits. Some suggested activities for younger children are presented in figure 1. Well-equipped visiting rooms and opportunities to talk about the parents' role in activities support parents in following through with many of these activities. Visit activities for older children and adolescents should reinforce their schoolwork and other interests. Certain parental behaviors support adolescents' development, such as setting firm but flexible limits, commenting positively about an adolescent's changing appearance, and supporting an adolescent in making decisions about his or her future.

Attention to the children's current developmental tasks in planning visits encourages parents to have reasonable expectations of their children. It also allows parents to assess their ability to parent, and it helps children to trust and gain confidence in their parents. All these factors are essential to successful reunification.

Children's Therapeutic Needs

Children's experiences in life or their special needs may also often determine visiting arrangements. For example, a girl who has been molested by her mother's boyfriend may at a point in her own treatment need to directly challenge her mother's denial of knowledge of the abuse. Visit planning during this period of her treatment should support her therapeutic tasks and anticipate her need for visit supervision, privacy, and flexibility in timing.

Physical therapy or medical treatment may limit children's mobility and thus the visit location. For example, some children are scheduled routinely for inpatient medical care or observation. Who will be allowed to visit during hospitalizations? If hospital visiting must be supervised, who will be responsible for arranging it? In addition, involving parents in the children's care during visits in the hospital, in the foster home, or in the parents' home may require that the parents be trained by the health care staff and that visits be supervised until the parents' ability to follow procedures appropriately can be assessed.

The therapeutic needs of children may also be prompted in part by the service goal and case activities. For example

Julie, age seven, and her nine-year-old sister, Janice, had been in foster care for three years and return home was not a feasible plan for them. The agency had petitioned for termination of their parents' rights. They continued to have supervised visits with their mother, but they were eager for their foster parents to adopt them, as the agency planned, and for contact with their mother to end. She was unpredictable and sometimes quite harsh. When the court ruled that the parents' rights be terminated, however, the children requested a final visit with their mother. Janice said they had things they wanted to tell her and they wanted pictures of the three of them together. The worker was very concerned about the mother's behavior toward the girls and about the direction the visit might take. It was clear, though, that the visit could have a therapeutic purpose in moving the girls into a permanent relationship with their adopting foster parents. With the assistance of the girls, the mother, and the foster parents, the worker planned a brief visit in an agency visiting room that was to focus upon picture taking. The visit included the foster parents, with whom the mother had had frequent contact, and the mother's best friend. The children made an audiotape for their mother with their messages to her and gave this to her at the visit, asking that she play it later. Thus, the children's need to express

Figure 1
Developmentally Related Visit Activities

Age	Developmental Tasks	Developmentally Related Visit Activities
Infancy (0–2)	Develop primary attachment	Meet basic needs (feeding, changing, holding, cuddling)
	Develop object permanence	Play peek-a-boo games
	Basic motor development (sit, reach, stand, crawl, walk)	Help with standing, walking, etc., by holding hand, play "come to me" games
	Word recognition	Name objects, repeat name games, read picture books
	Begin exploration and mastery of the environment	Encourage exploration; take walks; play together with colorful, noisy, moving items
Toddler (2–4)	Develop impulse control	Make and consistently enforce rules
	Language development	Read simple stories; play word games
	Imitation, fantasy play	Play "let's pretend" games; encourage imitative play by doing things together such as "clean house," "go to store"
		Play together at park; assist in learning to ride tricycle; dance together to music
	Small motor coordination	Draw together; string beads together
	Develop basic sense of time	Discuss visits and visit activities in terms of "after breakfast," "after lunch," "before supper," etc.
	Identify and assert preferences	Allow choices in activities, clothes worn, foods eaten

Age	Developmental Task	Parent/Caregiver Activities
Preschool / Early School (5–7)	Gender identification	Be open to discussing boy-girl physical differences
		Be open to discussing child's perception of gender roles; read books about heroes and heroines together
	Continuing development of conscience	Make and enforce consistent rules; discuss consequences of behavior
	Develop ability to solve problems	Encourage choices in activities
	Learning cause-effect relationships	Point out cause-effect and logical consequences of actions
	Task completion and order	Plan activities with beginning, middle, end (as prepare, make cake, clean up)
		Play simple games such as Candyland, Go Fish
	School entry and adjustment	Shop for school clothes together; provide birth certificate, medical record required for school entry; go with child to visit school, playground prior to first day; accompany child to school
School-age (8–12)	Skill development (school, sports, special interests)	Help with homework; practice sports together; demonstrate support of special interests, such as help with collections; attend school conferences and activities; work together on household tasks
	Peer group development and team play	Involve peers in visit activities
		Attend team activities with child (child's team or observe team together)
	Development of self-awareness	Be open to talking with child
	Preparation for puberty	Discuss physical changes expected; answer questions openly

their feelings and to have a good-bye ritual of taking pictures was met. Potentially hurtful dialogue was avoided by carefully structuring the visit location, length, and participants, and by closely supervising the visit.

Children's Schedules

Children's schedules include their ordinary daily routines of mealtimes, naptimes, playtimes, bathing, and bedtimes, as well as scheduled activities, such as school, treatment appointments, and clubs or lessons. Whenever possible, visits should be scheduled to involve parents in the children's routines, particularly when the children cannot return home until the parents are better able to provide ordinary daily care. Imagine a mother visiting with her eighteen-month-old son from 10:00 A.M to 11:30 A.M., after he has had breakfast and played and is ready for a nap. She is likely to be frustrated either because he sleeps through the visit or because he is thrown off his schedule and is fussy. It is better to schedule her visit earlier or later so that she can participate in a feeding and typical awake period.

You must anticipate and try to avoid creating problems in the child's usual routine by the way in which visits are scheduled. For example, foster parents often complain that children's appetites are spoiled by snacks provided by parents during after school visits. In many instances, however, deliberately scheduling visits to include a snack or meal provides an appropriate, routine focus for a part of the visit and places responsibility on parents to meet this basic need adequately. It also clarifies for caregivers that the children will not need to be fed immediately upon returning to the placement.

Beginning and ending visits at transition points already in children's schedules may ease the separation for them. For example, visits can begin immediately after school rather than later in the afternoon, or end when children go to school on Monday morning rather than on Sunday evening.

Scheduled activities should also be considered in planning visits. Older children, particularly, may resent missing an activity with their peers in order to visit. Not only should children not be denied participation in activities such as ball games or school activities that are important to them, but whenever possible their parents should be invited to participate in the activities with them. You should be vigilant to assure, however, that the schedules of placed children do not become too full for visits. While school activities and swimming, ballet, and piano lessons are important, placements where children's schedules have little room for visiting have to be looked into closely.

4

Case-Specific Considerations: Parents and Family Relationships

Visit planning is shaped by those parental behaviors and abilities that relate to the reason for placement and must change for the child to return home; that relate to the nature of the parents' cooperation in carrying out the visiting plan; and that endangered the child in visits during previous placements. Moreover, parents' requests regarding visiting arrangements, reactions to visiting, and schedules affect visit planning.

In some cases, the visiting plan will be the same for both parents. In many cases, the plan will be different. The difference may reflect the fact that one parent was not a custodial parent before placement or it may reflect a difference in the parent's interest in or treatment of the child. It is important that you consider each parent individually as well as consider the family relationships and interactions.

Parents' Behaviors and Abilities Related to Placement

The majority of children are placed due to parental actions or omissions that put them at grave risk, with reunification dependent on change in the parents' functioning. Visit planning gives specific attention to the situations that will promote and support that change. Visit arrangements, therefore, should vary somewhat depending upon the parents' behaviors that relate to the reason for placement.

Whatever the reason for placement, the parents' knowledge of the child's needs and the appropriateness of the parents' expectations of the child must be considered in planning visits. When parents' understanding of their children's needs is inadequate, including someone else in visits who can both model appropriate responses to the child and instruct the parents assures that parents are given ample opportunity to learn about the specific needs of their child.

Neglect
Placement may result from the parents' neglect of the child's physical,

37

emotional, or social needs; education; supervision; or medical care. Problems may exist with regard to housing and living conditions.

Visiting plans may vary in relation to the nature of and reasons for the parents' neglect. For example, if the parents are committed to, but unprepared for, parenthood, a comprehensive program of education, development of social supports, and resource mobilization may be indicated. Parents may participate in parenting courses and receive individualized instruction. In such instances, visits should allow the parents to care for the child in their own home with a home educator or other in-home services professional who instructs, provides feedback, models behaviors, and monitors the child's care. Visits must allow sufficient time for the parents to provide care in a realistic way. As the parents' abilities increase, so should the frequency and the length of visits.

If the parents' neglect reflects ambivalence about parenting in general or about parenting a particular child, the service will focus on helping parents to resolve their ambivalence and either commit themselves to parenting or work with the agency toward an adoptive placement or a placement with a relative. Visiting is also an essential component of this treatment process. Frequent, lengthy periods of time with the child help the parents confront their real feelings for the child, their willingness to be responsible for meeting the child's daily needs, and their ability to do so. With this group of parents, you must resist the temptation to succumb to a routine, weekly, hour-long visit. Ambivalent parents rarely ask for more, but routinized visiting prolongs indecision by providing an easy out for ambivalent parents: continued contact without responsibility.

If the neglect results from housing problems or problems primarily with living conditions related to poverty, every effort should be made to quickly find a place where children and parents can visit in ways that foster natural interaction. Neither extensive treatment nor supervision are indicated in such cases, and the primary, if not the only, function of visiting is to maintain the relationship between parents and children.

In cases where the parents reject children or are unwilling to assume parental responsibility, reunification may only briefly be the case goal. In such instances, contact should be closely supervised. If the visits are seen to be harmful to the child, the court's permission to limit or terminate the contact should be sought.

Physical abuse by parents

Abusive behaviors of parents may reflect inability to manage their own anger and impulses, limited awareness of effective child management techniques, or religious or philosophical commitment to corporal punishment. The nature, frequency, severity, and recency of the parents' abusing behaviors affect visit planning, particularly with regard to visit supervision and location. Planning is also affected by the parents' degree of acceptance of responsibility for their behaviors, and the progress made through rehabilitative efforts. As discussed previously, the child's age and capacity for self-protection are also critical considerations.

The planning of visiting for physically abusive parents requires the thoughtful input of all involved in the parents' treatment, as each change to increase the amount of contact and decrease the degree of supervision involves taking a carefully calculated risk. You have a right to expect the input and support of your supervisor and colleagues in making these difficult decisions.

Sexual abuse by parents

Caseworkers report that, particularly in sexual abuse cases, parents may pressure their child to recant allegations, and the abuser may continue to abuse the child. During the initial assessment period, therefore, close supervision is required to determine whether the parents accept or challenge the child's allegations and to determine whether inappropriate touching is likely to recur. Until it has been determined that each parent consistently behaves appropriately with the child, whoever is supervising the visit should not leave the child alone with a parent.

In some cases of sexual abuse the child is removed from the home. In others, the abusing parent is ordered from the home by the court. Even when the parent is ordered out of the home, the caseworker has the responsibility to develop a visiting plan that is consistent with the court's order for contact.

Parental failure to protect the child

A common reason for placement is abuse not by a parent, but by someone who is living with the family or who is a frequent visitor in the home. Such persons might include stepparents, friends, relatives, and babysitters. Placement results not because a parent has been abusive or even neglectful in terms of providing routine care and supervision, but because the parent is unable to protect the child. Reunification in such cases is contingent largely on the progress of the parent and the abuser in treatment or on the parent's ability to separate from the abuser. Similarly, home visits without supervision are contingent on the parent's ability to protect the child. Visiting must be supervised until it is clear that the parent can do so. In such cases, visiting in the foster home or visits in the homes of relatives can offer safety as well as a comfortable, natural setting that facilitates maintenance of the parent-child relationship.

Parental conditions

In some instances, the maltreatment of children directly arises from a parental condition that alters the parents' ability to care for or protect their child. The parents' mental health or chemical dependence may directly contribute to neglectful or abusive behaviors that endanger the child and that cannot be controlled without appropriate, sometimes lengthy, treatment. Poor physical health may also result in limitations or an inability to parent adequately.

Here, the management of the condition so that parents can resume responsibility for their children's care may be the service goal, rather than preparation for parenting. In some instances, particularly during the initial phase of placement, visits will necessarily be planned in collaboration with the parents' treatment staff. Clinicians may want to postpone or limit visits, based on the projected effects of visits on the parents' treatment. You will need to weigh their concerns against the children's need for contact and reassurance that they have not been abandoned.

As parents demonstrate a level of recovery from physical or mental illness or chemical dependence that allows them to resume parenting, you should consider the amount of time they spend with their child and the degree of stress that they can successfully manage. Monitoring the parents' compliance with their treatment program, such as regularly taking medication or attending AA, is the key to child protection when ability to parent depends on the control or management of a diagnosed condition.

Incarceration of a parent

Children are sometimes placed when a custodial parent is incarcerated and arrangements with other appropriate caregivers, such as extended family members, cannot be made. When a parent's incarceration is related to having harmed the child, the impact of contact with the parent on the child should be assessed. When a child is placed due to the parent's incarceration and family reunification is the goal, every effort should be made to assure regular visiting. The child's fantasy of the parent's experience in prison may be much more frightening than the reality, and visits can reassure the child that the parent is alive and safe.

In planning visits between children and incarcerated parents, it is essential to determine in advance what is required to secure permission for the child to visit, who can accompany the child to visits, and how often and for how long the child can visit. So that you can appropriately prepare the child, determine whether a child will be able to hug or kiss a parent or will be required to visit through a glass window, and what rules govern visit behaviors.

It is essential to examine your own attitudes about the child's visiting in prison. If you are uncomfortable with this plan, you may be depriving families of their right to contact by delaying the scheduling of visits.

Parents' Compliance with Visiting Plans

The extent of the parents' compliance with the visiting plan must be considered in visit arrangements. As emphasized earlier, visits are not planned to reward or punish parents for their cooperation or lack of it, but visit planning must take the parents' compliance into account.

Noncompliance may be examined at two levels: the actual behaviors and the meaning of the behaviors. Depending on the persistence and meaning of the noncompliance, your responses may differ. For example, parents might not cooperate with a plan for weekly visits at home, often not being there or always being late when the child is brought for the visits. This behavior might indicate an inability to keep track of the visit schedule, ambivalence about visits in the home and family reunification, worry about their own ability to care for or protect the child in the home, reaction to the pain of being separated from the child, disinterest in the child's return, and so forth. Each explanation suggests different actions for you to take.

Perhaps more common are parents who fail to keep scheduled visits in the office. Although this noncompliance might reflect lack of interest in the child or severe deficits in self-management, it could well be attributed to problems in arranging or paying for transportation or care for children still in the home, or extreme discomfort at simply being in the office. Office visits are awkward under the best of circumstances, and this awkwardness is increased when, as is the case in many offices, the visiting room is sterile and poorly furnished.

The reasons for lack of compliance with visit arrangements should always be explored. The lack of compliance might be due to problems with money, transportation, or child care; inability to tell time; changes in parents' work schedules; discomfort with the degree of responsibility given to them for the child's care; or simply misunderstanding of the arrangements. Eliminating such obstacles should always be tried before visit arrangements are modified.

When you determine that the apparent lack of cooperation is not the result of unreasonable expectations imposed by the agency or factors beyond the parents' control, and efforts to gain parental cooperation are unsuccessful, modifications in visit arrangements may be indicated. For example, if parents are consistently unavailable for visits in their home, a condition might be added to the visit plan requiring that they call to confirm that they are at home before the child is brought to the visit. Or, for a period of time, visits may be alternately scheduled in the foster home or at a location such as a park or fast food place, where the parents' failure to be consistently available has less impact on the use of agency resources, such as time for transporting, and where the child can be appropriately occupied while waiting.

When parents repeatedly fail to keep scheduled visits without good cause and despite your efforts to encourage visiting, a conference should be convened to discuss the visiting plan. Failure to visit is grounds for termination of parental rights in many states, and it may seem useful to continue to schedule visits that parents are unlikely to keep simply to *build* the case for termination. Before this course of action is taken, however, the staff must consider its effect on the children. To look forward week after week to seeing parents who do not appear can be devastating to children who are strongly attached to their parents. Because of the serious legal and psychological consequences of decision making at this point, the conference should include agency supervisory and legal staff members, the child's parents if at all possible, and if applicable, the child's therapist.

Parents' Past Endangering Behaviors

In some instances, you will have access to information regarding parents' visit-related behaviors during a previous placement. This information may be pertinent, particularly during the initial assessment phase. To illustrate: when records indicate that during a visit parents have tried to abduct a child; have threatened or tried to harm the child, agency staff members, substitute caregivers, or others; have been dishonest about harm that occurred during a visit; or have failed to ask for help when they recognized that they were in over their heads, the visit plan should include prohibitions against these behaviors, and arrangements to prevent them. Moreover, visit location, supervision, and participants should be planned to maximize the protection of all involved. Agency supervisory staff members should be involved in determining all visit arrangements in such cases.

Parents' Requests

Considering parents' requests about visit arrangements differs from developing a plan that provides for visits "at the parent's request." A plan that requires parents to request visits results in less frequent visiting than a plan that outlines visit arrangements. Plans for visits at the parent's request are therefore strongly discouraged. They ignore parents' and children's rights to contact as well as the role of planned visits in the treatment process. Only when the goal is not reunification, such as preparation for emancipation, should such a plan be considered.

It is essential that parents' preferences in visit arrangements be solicited and seriously considered. Solicited is a key word, as many parents hesitate to state their preferences. Parents may feel powerless and doubt your willingness to seriously consider their preferences; they may worry about irritating you and fear that their requests would result in less contact with their children. Don't assume that a lack of stated preferences reflects either a lack of motivation and interest in seeing their child, or agreement with the plan.

With parents, as with children, exploring the reason behind a request or stated preference is essential, since responding to the stated request may not effectively address the concern that prompted it. For example, one young mother requested that visits with her two children continue in the foster parents' home rather than be moved to her home as had been planned. Exploration revealed that she anticipated that when visits began in her home, her mother and sister would be critical of her care of the children and would take over, in contrast with the supportive way the foster parents had responded to her progress with the children. An intermediate step was planned. Two more visits were scheduled in the foster home, with the mother's own mother, sister, and the caseworker participating. This provided a chance for the mother's family to observe the improvements in her care of the children as well as to observe the caseworker's and foster parents' support. The visits also allowed for open discussion of the expectations of the mother and her family when the visits shifted to the children's home.

Parents' Reactions to Visits

Visits evoke a range of reactions in parents. "Visiting" is typically thought of as making a social call by appointment. The idea of visiting with one's own child, or having one's child visiting at home, stirs deep feelings for parents about themselves, their child, the substitute caregivers, and you. For example, a young mother of a four-year-old girl who had been in foster care about six months described her reactions this way: "I count the days to the next visit, but it rips my heart out to see her. She sees me as Mighty Mouse, thinking I can take her home, thinking I can make it happen, and I can't make it happen. It's hard not to be able to do what your child thinks you can." A father angrily described his reactions to visits: "There is never enough time. I dread coming. They make it hard on parents. They have all the power." Parents experience vulnerability, anger, and sadness, and are reminded of their failure as parents. Your empathy for parents and sensitivity to their feelings as a "visiting" parent will help you determine which arrangements are most comfortable.

Sometimes, parents' reactions to visiting distress the children and may also affect you, such as when parents promise repeatedly that they will take their child home the next time they see the child, or when parents are unwilling to end the goodbye embraces with their toddler. Whether you are disappointed, frustrated, or sympathetic in relation to parents, you must focus on their reaction, its meaning, and its impact on the child. Acknowledge the awkwardness, the pain, the discouragement, and the ambivalence that parents feel as they visit. Encourage them to talk with each other, with you, and with their therapists about their reactions to visits and how best to deal with their feelings.

When parents experience distress about ending visits and the separation following visits, an increase in visit frequency and duration should be considered as one way to relieve their distress. Extreme discomfort for parents visiting in the foster home, for example, may ultimately lead to making a change in visit arrangements. Before doing so, however, other interventions should be tried. Perhaps the foster mother is talking at length with a mother at each visit about the child's progress and success. The foster parent and the parent may hold radically different perceptions of this interaction. The mother may feel that the remarks are an implied criticism and infer disapproval; the foster mother may perceive the remarks as an important way to keep the mother informed about the child. In such instances, clarifying the perceptions and intentions may increase the foster parents' sensitivity and decrease the parents' discomfort.

It is realistic to expect that parents refrain from expressing their reactions inappropriately or in a manner hurtful to their children. When they do so, and efforts to help them react differently are unsuccessful, the visit plan should be revised either by identifying unacceptable behaviors in the plan or by revising other aspects of the plan.

Parents' Schedules and Accessibility

It is often difficult to find a visiting time that is convenient for all involved. Finding a time when parents are not working and can get child care, if necessary, for children at home, and locating the visit at a place easily accessible to the parents must be high priorities. The circumstance that many parents work at jobs with changing weekly schedules requires flexibility and creative planning of visits. Some parents, however, are either not employed, or have an employment status that allows them to request a specific work schedule. It is useful to talk directly with parents about visiting as both a right and a responsibility, emphasizing the importance of visiting for their child, for themselves, and as a part of the service plan. Making time for visits and use of other services must be a priority for parents during the placement period if the case goals are to be reached.

Parents sometimes decide to relocate and added distance becomes a major obstacle to regular, frequent visiting. At other times, the agency must place the child at a site that is remote from the parents. You and the parents should make every effort to continue visits as frequently as transportation can be arranged. Visits should be supplemented with regularly scheduled phone calls and letters.

Distance also may present an obstacle to visiting when parents are incarcerated. Some areas have volunteers that assist family members of inmates with visit arrangements and visit transportation. It is essential to determine whether visiting services are available.

As discussed in chapter 1, the agency's business hours may present a barrier to frequent visiting for some families. If you are finding this to be true, keep a record of the families whose need for visits at a specific time conflicts with agency hours. This information is needed to advocate successfully for changes in the agency's practice or for alternative service, such as purchase of visit supervision and transportation from another agency.

Family Relationships and Interactions

The visit plan is also shaped by the relationships of persons visiting together and by the nature of their interactions. Family is broadly defined to include persons living in the parents' household and acting as a member of the child's family, as well as those persons related to the child. Persons viewed by the child as family, whether or not the relationship is legally sanctioned by marriage or by adoption, should be included, at least periodically, in visits.

The assessment of family relationships and interactions helps decide (1) what frequency, length, and focus of visiting are necessary to maintain or build these relationships; (2) what degree of structure, including monitoring or supervising visits and selecting visit activities, is necessary to maintain a safe, manageable level of stress and conflict during visits; (3) what groupings of family members for visits will support the focus on parent-child interaction; and (4) what natural resources are available for assistance with transportation and supervision.

What visit arrangements will maintain or build relationships?

As discussed previously, maintaining and building family relationships constitute a fundamental purpose of visiting, whatever the placement phase. The child's age and sense of time strongly suggest the minimum visit frequency necessary to maintain these relationships for the child. When parents and children do not know each other well, do not like each other, or have an ambivalent relationship, visits should be planned with sufficient flexibility to allow an uncomfortable visit to end early or a good time to last longer. When children are getting to know a parent who has been absent, including someone else with the child in the visit whom the child already knows and trusts, such as an older sibling or foster parent, may provide important security.

Relationships among family members have been damaged in many cases by the experiences they have shared. When children consistently avoid physical or eye contact with a family member, seek distance from him or her, or convey discomfort in other ways, do not try to force hugs, sitting on laps, or other affectionate gestures during visits. Children must be allowed to rebuild relationships at their own pace. Parents may need your assistance in understanding this.

What visiting options will minimize stress and conflict?

The degree of conflict among members of the parents' household, divorced parents, or the extended family may sometimes limit your visiting options. Although conflict is definitely neither always negative nor always predictable, when there is reason to believe that family conflicts have the potential to escalate into emotional assault or physical violence, or when children are pulled into arguments among adults, visits should minimize that possibility. Consider selecting a more restrictive site for the visits, having the agency supervise the visits, or arranging separate visits for disputing parties. To illustrate:

> John's uncle lived in John's parents' home, helped with child care, and was close to John. Soon after John was placed, his father and uncle got into a fight that caused serious injuries to both, and John's uncle moved out. John wanted to visit with both his uncle and dad, and separate visits were planned. In another example, a mother who was wheelchair-bound was accompanied by her mother to the first two visits with her children. During each visit, the grandmother harshly criticized her daughter's care of the children to the point where the mother dissolved in tears. After discussing the situation, the caseworker and the mother planned

several visits at a time when the mother's sister, who was more supportive, could accompany her. In the interim period, the mother and grandmother agreed to meet with a family therapist to work on their conflictual relationship and its effect on the mother's parenting.

When it is evident that the combinations of family members involved in visiting create conflict and stress, you should consider a time-limited change in visiting arrangements to provide relief. For example, perhaps a mother with three sons in placement who is unable to adequately manage her two older sons' teasing and taunting of her youngest son could visit separately with the youngest and with his siblings, for several visits. This would allow her to tend to her relationship with her youngest son without the constant distraction and conflict created by the older boys' behavior. In such cases, counseling concerning the conflict should be provided. Conflict that is not addressed will be likely to continue and to affect the success of reunification.

What arrangements will increase parent-child interaction?

A focus on parent-child interaction during visits supports the primary purpose of visits, maintaining the parent-child relationship. You must be alert for instances where parent-child interactions are not the focus of visiting. For example, parents often ask to include a relative, boy/girlfriend, neighbor, or friend in visits. Is dad bored during visits and brings along a buddy? Does mom want her mother to come along to do the work of caring for a fussy infant? Or is dad bringing a friend who will join him in playing with his son? Is mom bringing her mother to show off her new-found ability to take care of her child?

Answers to questions such as these are critical, for children in placement fear abandonment and worry about rejection or that their parents will forget them. When their parents' attention during visits is consistently and primarily focused on someone else, children's self-esteem and sense of worth suffer.

Parents may also concentrate on one or two of their children to the exclusion of others—on the most troublesome child, the most verbal, or the youngest. Your knowledge of the family will help you decide whether, with your help, the parents can spread their attention more broadly; or whether, for a period of time, parents should visit with their children individually or in subgroups so that each child can share in the parents' attention.

Parents often interact with their children as if the latter were their peers, partners, or parents. A parent may burden the child with a list of problems and question: "What should I do? How can I manage without you?" When this happens, help the parent interact with the child more appropriately during visits by identifying the interactions as problematic, by helping the parent plan child-centered visit activities, and, if necessary, arranging for someone to supervise the visits. Services should also be addressing the problem of parent-child role reversal.

How can the family's social support network be tapped?

Parents may have friends or relatives who can help with visit transportation. Moreover, reliable relatives or friends may be sufficiently concerned about a child's well-being to supervise visits in their home or in the parents' home, with a clear agreement as to their role and responsibilities. This option is particularly useful during the latter part of the central phase and the reunification phase, when the parents' progress has decreased the risk to the child.

Friends and relatives can help parents care for their children during visits in the parents' home and reinforce parents in the parenting role. Although a friend or relative should not assume all or even primary responsibility for child care, we all know that parents in general often rely on friends and relatives for help with supervision and care and for advice, support, and validation. Why should we expect parents whose children are in care to assume sole responsibility during home visits? In fact, learning how to develop and appropriately use support networks is a major task of many parents whose children are in placement.

5

Case-Specific Considerations:
The Foster Parents

This chapter includes guidelines for determining how foster parents as caregivers might be involved in visits. In group care, the visiting plan will be influenced more by the policies of the facility than by your assessment of the substitute caregivers.

Agencies differ in their capacity to support foster parents' involvement in visits. Foster parents also differ significantly in their capacity and willingness to have contact with parents and to carry out different roles in visiting. Although foster parents cannot be allowed to determine whether children and parents will visit, foster parents can influence the nature of the contact that can take place between them and parents and the site of visits.

Agency Support of Foster Parents' Involvement
in Visiting

An essential consideration in planning visits is the amount of support the agency can provide to foster parents. Depending on the agency's licensing and training practices and the foster parents' experiences with the agency, foster parents' definitions of their role may vary. Where agencies see foster parents as team members who join with caseworkers and others in working toward a child's return home, foster parents are likely to define their role to include extensive personal contact with the child's family, and to have developed the capacity to do so. The opposite is true in agencies that do not define foster parenting in this way. The assessment of foster parent capacity for involvement with visits therefore covers not only individual capacity but also the agency's past and current contribution to the development of that capacity. If many of the children in your caseload are placed with foster parents who do not define involvement with the child's family as part of the foster parent role, changes in the agency's foster parent recruitment, licensing, and training program and in the agency's approach to teamwork are probably indicated.

A number of questions can be raised to assess your agency's support of foster parents' involvement in visiting. Can the agency reimburse foster parents for the costs of transportation and child care? Does the agency have a preservice and inservice education program that both instructs foster parents and provides them with an opportunity to share experiences with other foster parents? Do you have the time to listen to foster parents' concerns and to provide consultation and emotional support? If the answer to these questions is "yes," foster parents can be actively involved in visiting. If the agency cannot support foster parents' involvement in visiting, it is not reasonable to expect them to be active participants.

Foster Parents' Capacity to Support Reunification

Some foster parents can and should have extensive personal contact with the parents of a child who is in their care. Other foster parents, however, cannot work effectively with a child's parents and should have very limited contact. Your answers to the following questions will help you to determine foster parents' capacity to be involved in visiting.

What are the foster parents' attitudes toward parents?

While not necessarily condoning a particular parent's behavior, do the foster parents accept parents as persons and understand the stress they feel? Foster parents who accept children's parents can be helpful to parents; nonaccepting foster parents can undermine parents' confidence and efforts to change.

Do the foster parents value the child/parent relationship?

Foster parents who recognize and appreciate the importance of parents to their children will be able to share a child and to support the relationship between a child and his or her parents. Foster parents who do not value this relationship are likely to compete with parents and to undermine improvement in the child's relationship with the parents. Contact between such foster parents and the child's parents must be closely monitored.

Can the foster parents appropriately limit their relationship with the child's parents?

Foster parents must be able to differentiate their role from that of the parent's caseworker and therapist. It is not appropriate for them to try to counsel the child's parents or to make assurances to parents about the outcome of placement. Foster parents who are confident in their role as substitute caregivers and are able to restrict their relationship with parents consistent with this role can have contact without agency supervision.

Can the foster parents objectively record visit interactions ?

Foster parents should be encouraged to document actual visit interactions without allowing their own feelings about the parents and the children to interfere. In some instances, foster parents may need assistance in why they seem to emphasize parents' lack of progress one-sidedly. Foster parents who can objectively observe and record visit interactions can be a valuable resource for supervising visits.

Can the foster parents intervene as necessary?

Some foster parents are assertive and able to intervene with parents as needed. Other foster parents are fearful and hesitant in their interactions with parents. To illustrate: parents who abuse alcohol may have as a condition of visiting that they be sober during visits. If a foster parent is comfortable in refusing to allow an apparently intoxicated parent to take a child from the foster home for a visit, the plan can allow the parent to pick the child up at the foster home. If a foster parent is not comfortable saying "no," plans must be made to have the parent meet the child at another place.

Will the foster parents maintain confidentiality?

All foster parents are expected to hold confidential any information concerning children and their parents. People differ, however, in their ability to do this. Moreover, visiting raises some special issues concerning confidentiality. Visiting is both a public and private event. Not everything that occurs during a visit should be reported to you. Family conversations that do not relate to the plan for the child or reflect progress or lack of progress need not be repeated to you. As the placement continues, much of the interaction between child and parents can, and should be, private. Two questions, therefore, that arise in determining whether foster parents can supervise visits or be involved in visits are (1) can they resist sharing information with persons outside the agency? and (2) can they discern what you should be told and what can remain private?

What are the foster parents' resources?

Visiting is demanding on all participants and can be costly in terms of time and physical and emotional energy. The extent to which foster parents can be involved in visiting depends in part on their resources. Do they have the time to provide transportation? Do they have the time to supervise visits or to teach parenting skills during visits? Do they have the physical and emotional energy to be involved frequently with children's parents?

The answers to these questions reflect not only the foster parents' characteristics, but also agency demands imposed on the foster parents. If foster parents have only one child, or the children from only one family, they will have more resources to devote in support of visiting. If they have children from several families in placement, their resources will be spread more thinly. They cannot be as helpful with visits as you and they might want.

Some cases are less demanding than others. If the case is unusually difficult for whatever reason, the foster parents' resources will be more quickly strained; they may not be able to be as actively involved in visiting as you might wish.

Money is a resource that is often overlooked in considering how foster parents might be involved in visiting. Agencies usually reimburse foster parents for the costs they incur in support of visiting. It is a problem when agencies do not reimburse foster parents for these expenses or when foster parents have to wait for several weeks to be reimbursed. This problem can be significant when visits are frequent and the visit distances are great.

Can the foster parents be flexible and tolerate stress?

Parents of children in placement often are disorganized and unpredictable. The extent to which foster parents can manage this will determine in part the extent to which they can be involved in visiting.

Can the foster parents recognize their need for assistance?

Visiting stirs complex feelings in foster parents, particularly at the beginning of placement when they may feel outrage at how a child was treated, and as the time for reunification nears when they are confronted with feelings of loss. Moreover, events occur in visits that may necessitate a request for the agency's assistance. The extent to which foster parents can interact personally with parents during and surrounding visits without your involvement will be influenced by their ability to request assistance appropriately and to use the assistance and consultation that you provide.

Foster Parents' Willingness to Assist with Visiting

It is evident that foster parents' unwillingness to assist with visiting may affect their usefulness as a placement resource. A foster parent's willingness to assist with visiting should, therefore, be considered in licensing and placement decisions. Some foster parents have personal qualities that could make them a valuable resource in working toward reunification, but for a variety of reasons, are unwilling to be involved in visiting in certain ways.

All foster parents should be expected to help prepare the child for visits and to accommodate to reasonable visiting plans. Foster parent applicants who are not willing to do so should not be licensed. Unless there is agency policy to the contrary, however, foster parents have the right to refuse to allow visits in their home and to refuse to supervise visits or to teach parenting skills during visits. You therefore need to assess the foster parents' willingness to allow visits in their home; to supervise visits in their home or elsewhere, and to document what occurs as requested; and to teach a parent how to provide special care that the child might need. How much of the transportation are they willing to provide?

When you discover after a child has been placed that foster parents are unwilling to be involved in visiting, you should initially assume an educational role. Describe the purposes of visiting, stress the importance of their commitment to visiting, and reassess with them what they are willing to do. If the foster parents modify their reactions and accommodate to reasonable visiting plans, visiting services should be sought to supplement their involvement. If, after further discussion they are still unwilling to be involved in visiting, it is unlikely they will be supportive of other reunification efforts. Disruption of the placement must then be considered.

Foster Family's Schedule

The visit plan must also take the foster family's schedule into account. If a foster parent is expected to comfort a child following a visit, the plan must assure that he or she is home when the child returns from a visit, rather than have the child returned by a parent or a volunteer at a time when it is known that a foster parent will not be home and an older child or someone else will be receiving the child. Similarly, visit beginnings and endings should not be scheduled at times that will be highly disruptive for the foster family, such as the family's regular dinner hour.

Visits on holidays or during vacation periods require particularly thoughtful advance planning in order to minimize confusion for the child and disruption to the foster family. When possible, visits to the child's home should be scheduled to begin and end at natural transition points, such as at the end of the school day before Thanksgiving rather than during Thanksgiving morning, to ease the separation for the child and decrease disruption for the foster family.

Impact of Visiting on Other Children in the Home

A final consideration related to the foster family is the impact of visiting on other children in the home. As in the case of foster parents' capacity and willingness to participate in visiting, the impact on other children cannot preclude visits but it may influence the site of visits and other visit arrangements.

How distressing are one child's visits to other children in the foster home?

Many foster parents care for children from more than one family at a time. Moreover, many foster parents have biological children and many have adopted former foster children. One child's visits can have a powerful effect on other children in the family, either foster, adopted, or biological. One child's visits may generate both positive and negative reminders for other children of their own parents. It is easy to overlook the effect of one child's visits on other children in the home. If visiting in the foster home or if contact between the foster family and one child's parents appears to be having a detrimental effect on another child, consideration must be given to changing arrangements.

Does support of one child's visits result in neglect of other children in the home?

In their desire to be helpful foster parents may commit themselves to more than they can realistically do. They may not recognize the signs of overcommitment until it is too late—until they become impatient with all the children in the home or until a child in the home manifests new problematic behavior. When they recognize that they cannot give sufficient attention to one child because of the demands that another child imposes, they may not tell you out of fear that you will think they are inadequate and will move a child. You must be alert to the balance of attention the children are receiving and make other visiting arrangements if it appears that one child's visiting plan is resulting in lack of attention to other children in the home.

6

Preparing for and Coordinating Visits

When you have a visiting plan that is closely related to the service plan, reflects the case goal, and takes the specifics of the child's situation into account, your task is well begun, but in a sense, just half-done. The plan that you have carefully developed or recently revised is not likely to be followed unless you are actively involved in preparing the child, family members, and substitute caregivers for visits, in coordinating visiting arrangements, and in continually evaluating the visits that take place. This chapter discusses these tasks as well as the documentation of visits.

Questions for All Persons Involved in Visiting

All persons directly involved in visiting should have complete, current information about visiting arrangements and regular opportunities to talk about visiting and the feelings stirred by visiting. Each person should also have regular opportunities to discuss the following explicit questions with you.

What is the current visiting plan?

This includes information about the frequency, length, and location of visits, and whether and by whom they will be supervised. Who will participate in arrangements for transportation, activities during visits, required or prohibited behaviors, and how changes in visiting arrangements can be made must also be addressed.

How am I and others likely to react to visits?

We all find it useful to know what to expect when we are facing a difficult situation. This is certainly true with visiting, an event that for most parents and children is initially extremely awkward and emotionally charged. Knowing something about typical responses to visits can help participants prepare for and cope with their own reactions. The result will be more rewarding and productive visits. For example, parents who know that during the early part of visits many children act as if they are angry with their parents or shy away from their parents are less likely to take this behavior personally and respond in kind than parents who expect children to respond warmly.

Because feelings concerning placement and visiting are intense, it may be tempting to avoid discussing common negative reactions to visits, to reassure those involved that "everything will be okay." Everything during visits may not be okay, and certainly most children and their families will not be feeling okay, particularly early in the placement. Such statements, therefore, fail to validate family members. Moreover, because these reassurances have no foundation, they may not only be misleading, they may also block effective communication between you and family members. They may also undermine the parent-child relationship by creating false expectations and disappointment.

What is expected of me during visits?

Clarify the role and responsibilities of each person participating in visits and discuss planned visiting activities. This decreases the awkwardness of visits and increases the likelihood that visiting activities will contribute to progress in the service plan. Part of your responsibility is to teach family members and others what is expected of them and how best to make visits meaningful and purposeful.

What are my options for handling visit-related problems?

Most visit participants, at least at some point in the process, have worries and fears about visiting: "What if . . . ?" What if she doesn't return him on time? What if he acts up and won't mind me? What if my mom leaves me? The list of "what if?" questions can be lengthy. Identifying and thinking through the "what if?" questions may decrease anxiety, and more importantly, may enable participants to prevent difficult or dangerous situations or handle them should they occur.

Whenever possible, you, the parents, older children, and the substitute caregivers should meet together to review visit arrangements and visit-related responsibilities and expectations. Discussion with all persons involved may prevent misunderstandings and problems. Should problems arise later, this discussion, especially if documented, serves as a point of reference and helps in confronting "no one told me" complaints.

Working with Children

Immediately following placement, or before placement if the placement has been planned, the questions listed above should be discussed with children. In the initial phase of the placement, preparing children for visiting should focus on their anxieties and fears concerning being with their parents and the limits on contact that are imposed. Must they stay in the office? Will they not see someone they expect to see? Recognize that it is normal for children to be nervous, ambivalent, and confused about visiting, and preoccupied with details. Who will pick me up? Where will it be? Will I be home for lunch? Since younger children have difficulty with time, the days of the week and phrases such as "for an hour" have little meaning. Use instead the child's understanding of schedule, such as before or after lunch, while Sesame Street is on, or on the day Billy and Susie don't go to school. Providing an individual calendar with visiting days marked helps school-age children keep track of the visiting schedule.

Help children become aware of their feelings and talk about them. You might say something like "Some children feel nervous and some are real excited. How about you?" Or "Some children get upset when they say goodbye as visits end, but some children are glad." Or "After visiting, some children feel mad or lonely. It helps to talk about your feelings." Where a child's concern for personal safety can be anticipated, describe what the person supervising the visit will do if necessary to protect the child.

Whenever possible, elicit the child's fantasy of what visiting will be like, then correct misinformation, respond to feelings, and think through the "what if?" questions together. Using play or drawings to help children communicate their ideas and feelings about visiting is often useful. You might use dolls to illustrate a fictional story about children in placement who visit their parents, describing important things such as place, participants, the role of the visit supervisor, and the children's worries and reactions. You and the child might read a book together about a child in placement. Or you might ask children to draw pictures of what they imagine visiting will be like, what they wish it would be like, or what they are worried it will be like, and use the drawings as a means for the children to talk about their fantasies and questions.

Children are often reassured to know that other children are in foster care and visiting their parents and that these children have many of the same reactions to visits. Encouraging discussion about visiting among siblings in placement or among a group of children recently placed decreases the child's sense of isolation and being different and may prompt discussion about concerns they might not have brought up individually.

As the placement progresses into the central and reunification phases, preparing for visits occurs along with the processing and evaluation of previous visits. What happened? How did it feel? What should continue the same? What should be changed? In most instances the child's preparation for visits during these phases also occurs in discussions with the child's therapist and substitute caregiver.

As agency supervision of visits decreases, discuss thoroughly with the child the indicators that a visiting situation might be becoming volatile or dangerous. Develop a plan that the child can follow should she or he need to call for help or get away from the situation. Practice the required skills, such as dialing the number where you or other designated persons will be available to the child. Developing the child's age-appropriate self-care and protection skills is an essential aspect of visit preparation as reunification approaches.

If it is determined that family reunification is not possible, children need assistance in understanding the alternate permanent plan, why they cannot return home, and the nature of the relationships they will have with family members in the future. The child will need your help in dealing with the reality of changing or ending family relationships and with any resulting changes in visiting. Children must know when contact with their parents and other family members will be limited or ended. Help them plan what they would like to do, say, or ask in final visits. Explore what would support them in coping with these vital happenings in their lives. What is not worked through now will handicap their emotional growth.

Working with Family Members

Parents must also have regular opportunities to explore the four questions set forth earlier in this chapter. In the initial phase of the placement, the preparation of parents should also cover several additional areas. First, stress how important parents are to their children. Initially after placement, many parents feel blamed, worthless, or defensive. A clear message as to their value and importance to their children is both affirming and encouraging.

Second, discuss the pull to avoid visiting that many parents experience because of the awkwardness, anger, numbness, or sadness they feel or expect to feel upon seeing their child. Ways to deal with feelings and reactions other than avoiding visits should be discussed.

Third, point up parents' rights and responsibilities with regard to visiting. Describe the agency's intention to provide regular, frequent visiting and the parents' and child's right to it. Strongly emphasize parents' responsibility to visit. Discuss the insult children experience when their parents do not visit and children's fears of being abandoned by their parents. Make clear that visiting is the principle means for parents to protect their relationship with their child during placement and that visiting has a central role in your work with them toward the child's return home. Moreover, parents must be informed explicitly of the possible legal consequences of their failure to visit. In other words, help parents understand how necessary visiting is and convey a clear, nonambiguous message: You expect the parents to visit and will work with them to develop and carry out a visiting plan.

Fourth, prepare parents for their children's behavior during visits, such as clinging and crying or anger and withdrawal; reassure parents that many children in placement, not just theirs, behave in unexpected ways during visits, and provide suggestions about handling these behaviors.

Fifth, spell out the various functions that persons supervising visits may have, including helping parents learn to deal with children's behaviors, recording changes and progress in the family interactions, and setting limits on behaviors that could become hurtful. Make sure that the parents know that the visit supervisor will report to you concerning what he or she observes.

Finally, when germane, make clear the agency's and the court's expectations that the parents will not pressure children to recant their allegations of abuse and identify any other visit-related behaviors that the agency has concluded must be required or prohibited in each case.

As the placement progresses, working with parents on visiting increasingly involves evaluating previous visits and planning subsequent ones. Planning visit activities suited to the child's current developmental tasks, as described in chapter 3, allows for teaching and for emphasizing the importance of parent-child interactions during visits.

When parents do not visit as arranged, it is essential that you contact them immediately to determine why the visiting appointment was not kept. This is consistent with your statement to them that you expect them to fulfill their responsibility to visit. Reemphasize the importance of visiting for their child's well-being and for reunification. Identify any obstacles to visiting that may exist and explore any reactions the parents have to visiting that may be affecting their compliance with the plan.

Throughout the placement, working with parents on visiting addresses the parents' feelings about each child in placement and about the plan for reunification. Your attention to parents' reactions to visits and to preparing parents for visits and evaluating visits is essential. Discussions with parents about their visits and the assessment of the feasibility and timing of the child's return home are closely related. Be watchful for indications of parental ambivalence about reunification so that worries, questions, and feelings can be explored. In some instances, sensitive exploration of ambivalence may over time lead to a parent's decision to voluntarily surrender parental rights.

Persons other than parents who visit, including nonplaced siblings and unrelated members of the parents' household, should also be prepared for visiting. Explain the purposes of visiting and the expectation that during visits the parents are responsible for their children's care and supervision. Specify that visiting family members are expected to support, not interfere with, the parents' involvement with their child.

Working with Foster Parents and Other Substitute Caregivers

Foster parents are usually with their foster children before and after each visit and, in many instances, visits are located at the child's placement and monitored by the foster parents. Continuing discussions with substitute caregivers about visiting are vital. As noted in the introduction to this guide, the majority of children in placement are cared for by foster parents, but substitute caregivers also include relatives providing placement and staff members in group homes and other residential facilities. Although we refer primarily to foster parents in this section, the discussion applies to all persons providing substitute care.

Like children and parents, foster parents and others providing substitute care need regular opportunities to discuss the following questions with you:

What is the current visiting plan?

What can I expect in terms of my own and other's reactions to visiting?

What should I do during visits? What is expected of me?

How should I handle visit-related problems? What are my options if I need assistance?

Unlike children and parents, foster parents may have had opportunities to review in training sessions the purposes of visiting and their involvement in visiting. Some caregivers have had extensive training or experience with visiting. In these instances, your discussions can focus primarily on the visit plan for the particular child and family, how the foster parents will help carry out the plan, and the reactions and questions that the foster parents have.

If the foster parents have not participated in training or if they have had previous negative experiences with visiting, your work may be cut out for you. Describe the purposes of visiting and stress the importance of the foster parents' commitment to visiting. You may want to enlist a foster parent who has had positive experiences with visiting as a resource or consultant to the foster parents during the child's placement. If your agency does not provide training and reading materials on visiting for foster parents, you may want to discuss the need for this with your supervisor and with other agency staff members.

You should help foster parents or other substitute caregivers think about visiting from the child's and parents' points of view. Discuss together what you both might do to decrease their discomfort. For example, if several visits are to be located in the foster parents' home, what would best facilitate natural interaction between parent and child, encourage parental responsibility for the child's care and supervision during the visit, and provide appropriate privacy? When visits are located elsewhere and the parent is coming for the child, should the foster parent walk the child to the car or invite the parent to come in? What should be ready for the child to take to visits away from the foster home—formula, clothes, toys?

As noted in chapter 5, foster parents may assume different roles and responsibilities with regard to visiting depending on the service plan; the child's needs; the parents' feelings, attitudes, and behaviors; and the foster parents' capacity, skills, training, and attitudes. In support of visiting, however, all foster parents are expected to:

> cooperate with the visiting plan, including assisting with transportation, recording visit-related information, and permitting the child to spend special days with parents;

> encourage the child's open expression of feelings about visiting;

> maintain confidentiality about the child and the child's family;

> avoid demeaning the parents to the child or to others; and

> discuss their own reactions to visiting arrangements with you, not with the child or parents.

In most cases, visits at some point during the placement will be held in the foster home. Other activities in which both the parents and the foster parents may participate would include school conferences, clinic appointments, and so forth. In many cases foster parents will provide additional services, such as helping parents develop parenting skills through teaching and modeling. Whatever the agreement regarding the foster parents' role and responsibilities in visiting, your availability to them to plan, process, advise, interpret, and mediate is essential to the plan's success. Foster parents must be encouraged to identify and record progress that they observe. Problems that arise should be dealt with quickly and directly.

In your discussion with foster parents regarding visiting, try to anticipate the problems that might arise and discuss possible responses. Foster parents should be encouraged to contact you as soon as possible when:

parents do not keep visiting appointments or try to visit at unscheduled times;

parents come for visits late, very distressed, intoxicated, or with persons who don't have permission to visit;

parents behave in ways that upset their child or other children in the home;

parents refuse to end visits or consistently return the child from visits later than agreed;

the child consistently tries to avoid visiting or ending visits;

the child is distressed by visiting or some aspect of the visiting arrangements; or

other observations suggest visit-related difficulties.

Much of the discussion up to this point suggests that the interaction between foster parents and a child's parents is always problematic, but foster parents who are committed to reunification and who view themselves as important agents in achieving reunification typically derive a great deal of satisfaction from their work with parents. Their contributions are often overlooked, however. They need and deserve your encouragement, recognition, and suggestions concerning their work.

Working with Others Providing Visit-Related Services

Persons providing visit-related services such as transportation, supervision, or individualized parent education also need adequate preparation to fulfill their responsibilities. It is important to provide sufficient information without adding case information that is not germane to their role, and that might violate confidentiality.

Persons who transport family members to visits must have accurate information about time and place, best route, how long to wait, need for a child or infant car seat, most workable seating arrangements in the car for siblings, and anticipated behavior management problems and methods to deal with them. It is important to develop a way of promptly getting the transporter's observations of the children and any other information that might affect subsequent visit planning.

Persons supervising visits need to know the particular purpose of their supervision. As discussed earlier, supervision as we use the term has many purposes. Is the purpose primarily child protection? Is the purpose to provide instruction? Does the supervisor need to assess the current functioning of a family member or the whole family? How important is documentation of the visiting interactions? Whatever the purpose, visit supervisors need information concerning the reason for placement and the service plan. They also need information about difficulties that may arise during the visit and preferred methods for resolving difficulties. They need to know under what circumstances visits should be ended prematurely and who will be available if assistance is needed. In addition, the agency's requirements for documentation should be spelled out and forms provided, if necessary. A plan for follow-up with persons supervising visits is essential so that you can have the benefit of their observations.

As in the case of foster parents, volunteers and professional staff members who provide visit-related services need and deserve recognition of their efforts and feedback concerning their work. This is particularly true regarding volunteers and homemakers who, unlike professionally educated staff members, often lack confidence and are uncertain about how to evaluate their own performance. Moreover, volunteers receive no pay, and the salaries of homemakers are typically very low. Your thanks and suggestions can be powerful motivators to keep them involved in providing services.

Coordinating and Evaluating Visiting Arrangements

Coordination and evaluation of visiting arrangements are necessary to facilitate the harmonious working of all involved toward the same end. Coordination and evaluation include several responsibilities:

development of the visiting plan;

preparation of those involved for visits, including convening meetings of persons involved as necessary to clarify roles, expectations, and arrangements;

provision of needed visit-related services such as service transportation or day care or referral for such services;

monitoring compliance of all parties with the visiting plan;

monitoring the consistency between visit arrangements and agency policy and court orders;

constant assessment of the appropriateness of the visiting plan given case phase and progress;

timely revision of the plan;

mediation of conflicts that arise related to visiting;

advocacy in behalf of children and families when obstacles to visiting are created by agency practices or when visit-related services to which they are entitled are not available, not provided, or of poor quality; and

assuring that an agency supervisor is aware of and involved in decision making related to visiting and is alerted to problems and difficulties that are expected or that occur unexpectedly.

To effectively coordinate and evaluate visiting, you will need firsthand knowledge of how the arrangements are being carried out. Even if other arrangements are available, providing transportation or periodically monitoring visits yourself is necessary to evaluate not only the family's interaction but also how visiting arrangements are being carried out by substitute caregivers and other service providers. Meeting every four to six weeks with all the parties to visiting in a given case helps to exchange information, to identify and resolve problems, and to encourage appropriate changes in the plan. At a minimum, the plan must be reviewed with all participants as part of the regularly scheduled case review.

Documentation of Visits

Because visiting is an essential element of the agency's service to families, accurate records must be maintained regarding the visit plan and its revisions, the family's involvement in visiting, and the visit-related services provided. Some agencies require that substitute caregivers maintain a log recording visit dates, time of visits, participants, interactions they observe, and the child's reactions following the visit. Although all persons providing visit-related services have direct observations to record, it must be clear where and by whom the agency's official records of each child's visits are maintained. Many agencies have designed a form or logsheet to increase consistent recording of visit-related case information.

Another aspect of documentation is often overlooked—maintaining records concerning visit-related service needs and obstacles to visiting. If you are to identify service needs effectively and advocate in behalf of children and families served by your agency, it is necessary for you, your supervisor, and others in your agency to maintain a listing of needed unavailable services, of agency placement practices that result in visit-related difficulties (such as distance of placement), and a record of the number of clients affected.

7

Visiting and Your Self Care

As described in chapter 1, visits can place enormous stress on you. You observe the distress of children and parents. You may feel vulnerable professionally as you make judgments about the safety of children. You may feel personally vulnerable when parents become threatening or hostile. You may struggle to keep your professional and personal lives balanced as you find yourself scheduling visits beyond your agency's hours on your own time to accommodate parents' schedules, or find yourself preoccupied over the weekends or holidays with concern about children who are having extended visits at home.

If you are to maintain your commitment to visiting in the face of the demands it imposes and carry out this commitment competently, caring for yourself is vital. There are several types of stress-producing problems that, when recognized, can be ameliorated. These include failure to use fully those resources that are available to support your work related to visiting, difficulties in management of caseload and time, and difficulties in recognizing and asserting one's professional and personal limits. Suggestions concerning each of these are discussed briefly below.

Using Available Resources

Identify the resources your agency does provide to support your work in relation to visiting and ask yourself: Am I using these resources to the fullest or carrying more of the load alone than is necessary? The resources include not only the persons available to provide visit-related services but also supervision, case conferences, and team meetings where visit plans and concerns can be reviewed and discussed. Most workers find that shared decision making reduces the sense of vulnerability and stress that accompany difficult visit decisions. Sometimes workers hesitate to use case conferences or team meetings for fear of self-exposure, or of losing some of the autonomy they have in visit planning. The benefits, however, are substantial. Groups generate creative resolutions to problems and provide a broad base of information to draw from, as well as a shoulder to lean on.

Another agency resource that supports your work in visits is flextime or comp time. The demands of planning, scheduling, and supervising visits while also meeting other appointments often make it seem as if your schedule is out of your hands and out of control. Take a look at your calendar for the past three months. Have you been using flextime to adjust your professional schedule? Have you claimed allowable compensated time to balance out the additional visit-related work hours? Are you using your vacation time to detach yourself periodically from your work and replenish yourself? Or have you become resigned to losing comp time or saving an unreasonable number of unused vacation days because you "don't have the time" to claim your time? Protecting your personal time and life by claiming the time benefits your agency provides is essential to self-care.

If your agency is short on supportive resources for visiting, identify those that are not provided and develop a strategy for obtaining them. For example, if your agency does not provide for flexibility in your work time to schedule visits according to clients' needs, begin to document the instances in which this has barred regular, frequent visiting and assert the need for this change in your clients' and your own behalf. Your supervisor and colleagues can be allies in documenting needs for visit-related services, for greater variation in agency hours, and for agency policies and practices that support visiting across caseloads.

Management of Caseload and Time

Agency assignments of homogenous caseloads and poor time management also contribute to workers' stress levels. Review your caseload with your supervisor. Is there variation within it (ages of children, permanency plans, reason for placement), or are you serving a homogenous caseload with characteristics that present visit scheduling problems for you? For example, are many of your children placed at some distance from home, requiring extensive visit transportation? Are most of the children in your caseload of school age, requiring afterschool visits during the academic year? Variety within caseloads contributes to greater flexibility in scheduling visits, particularly supervised visits, and decreases the cynicism or boredom that can be a reaction to carrying a full caseload of similar cases.

Books and workshops on time management offer consistent advice, including directives to set and use priorities to determine your daily schedule; to delegate; to regularly schedule uninterrupted time periods for activities that require concentration; and to determine what investments in time will pay off in time saved. A time-management principle in visiting is that a heavy investment in time on the front end for planning and preparation of persons involved will decrease problems and save time as the placement progresses. There are variations on this theme. For example, time spent in locating and preparing reliable, competent resource persons to provide visit transportation or supervision is an investment that will free up your time for case activities that cannot be delegated, and free you from the concern that you will be forced to choose between assisting with a child's visit and dealing with a crisis in another case.

Recognizing and Asserting Limits

Workers often contribute to their visit related stresses by not recognizing and asserting their own limits. Limitations involve not only those of time and schedule, but also some more personal in nature. For example, one stress-producing limit that must be recognized and confronted is that of professional expertise. You may feel insufficiently prepared to make the decisions described in this book, to prepare persons for visits, or to supervise specific visits. You have a right to expect your agency to provide orientation and training about your work and to provide a supervisor who is knowledgeable and available to discuss visit decisions and planning with you. In instances where supervision of visits could involve a risk to you, you have a right to supervisory involvement in developing a plan that protects you as well as your clients.

Another stress-producing limit is a temporary or persistent inability to cope with the steady exposure to intense feelings and reactions related to family relationships that visiting requires. If you have had or are in the midst of personal experiences rather like those of your clients, you may find yourself overidentifying with either parents or children in visiting situations, focusing on your own current situation or memories rather than on your clients' situations, or losing sight of the agency's service mandates and under- or overinvesting in service to particular clients. If this is occurring, it is important to talk with your supervisor, a colleague, or a counselor to sort through how your reactions or sensitivity to the clients' situations may be affecting your professional performance and your own well-being. Resolving personal matters directly rather than through your clients is a professional responsibility. In such instances a temporary shift in work responsibilities should be explored with your supervisor.

Workers often describe their attraction to the challenge, the importance, the pace, and the diversity of child welfare work. Stress is inherent however, in this work generally, and a constant in visit-related activities.

No matter what supports agencies provide, most workers experience periods of increased stress. It is necessary, therefore, to learn to monitor your own stress level and to use those methods of stress-reduction you find useful. There are many resources that describe the indicators that job-related stress is reaching a level that is affecting your well-being and performance. Recognizing your own personal distress indicators and intervening in your own behalf is essential. You must care for yourself if you are to care for others.

Bibliography

Blumenthal, K., and Weinberg, A. "Issues Concerning Parental Visiting of Children in Foster Care." In *Foster Children in the Courts*, edited by M. Hardin. Boston, MA: Butterworth Legal Publishers, 1983, pp. 372–398.

Fanshel, D., and Shinn, E. *Children in Foster Care: A Longitudinal Investigation.* New York: Columbia University Press, 1978.

Hess, P. "Case and Context: Determinants of Planned Visit Frequency in Foster Family Care." *Child Welfare* LXVII, 4 (July–August 1988): 311–326.

———. "Parent-Child Attachment Concept: Crucial for Permanency Planning." *Social Casework* 63, 1 (January 1982): 46–53.

Hess, P., and Proch, K. "How the States Regulate Parent-Child Visiting." *Public Welfare* 44, 4 (Fall 1986): 12–17.

Proch, K., and Hess, P. "Parent-Child Visiting Policies of Voluntary Agencies." *Children and Youth Services Review* 9, 1 (1987): 17–18.

Proch, K., and Howard, J. "Parental Visiting of Children in Foster Care: A Study of Casework Practice." *Social Work* 31, 3 (May/June 1986): 178–181.

———. "Parental Visiting in Foster Care: Law and Practice." *Child Welfare* LXIII, 2 (March–April 1984): 139–147.

Weinstein, E. *The Self-Image of the Foster Child.* New York: Russell Sage Foundation, 1960.

The Authors

Peg McCartt Hess, Ph.D., ACSW, is Associate Professor, Indiana University School of Social Work, Indianapolis, IN. Since 1983, she has coordinated a collaborative project between the Indiana University School of Social Work and the Indiana State Department of Public Welfare, developing and delivering training for child welfare caseworkers, supervisors, and foster parents. Dr. Hess has also provided direct services and supervised social work staff in several family and children's services agencies. She teaches primarily in the areas of social work practice and research.

Kathleen Ohman Proch, Ph.D., is Associate Professor, Graduate School of Social Work, University of Denver, Denver, CO. Her research has focused on placement disruption, parental visiting of children in out-of-home care, and adoption. Her interest in these areas grew out of her experience as a protective services worker with the Illinois Department of Children and Family Services. Dr. Proch teaches primarily in the areas of law and social welfare policy.